INSIGHT FROM

THE Style Guy

Dating: "If you want to see her again, just tell her sincerely how much you enjoyed yourself and that you'd like to do it again. If you don't want to see her again, just tell her insincerely how much you enjoyed yourself and leave it at that."

How can I convince my girlfriend to wear spike heels? They really turn me on. Confess your fetish and tell her if she doesn't start wearing them you will.

Going bald: "I don't think baldness is such a big deal. It's trying to hold on to what you ain't got that's unattractive."

Clip-on bow ties: "They should only be worn if they contain a water-squirting device."

D1564068

THE Style Guy

GLENN O'BRIEN

THE ANSWERS TO THE QUESTIONS
MEN ARE ASKING ON SEX, MANNERS,
GROOMING, FASHION, TRAVEL,
WOMEN, AND THE MEANING OF LIFE.

BALLANTINE BOOKS • NEW YORK

A Ballantine Book
The Ballantine Publishing Group

Copyright © 2000 by Glenn O'Brien
Illustrations copyright © 2000 by Steven Salerno

All rights reserved under International and Pan-American Copyright Conventions. Published in the United States by The Ballantine Publishing Group, a division of Random House, Inc., New York, and simultaneously in Canada by Random House of Canada Limited, Toronto.

Ballantine and colophon are registered trademarks of Random House, Inc.

Grateful acknowledgment is made to Farrar Straus & Giroux, LLC, for permission to reprint an excerpt from *A Picnic Cantata* from *Selected Poems* by James Schuyler. Copyright © 1988 by James Schuyler. Reprinted by permission.

STYLEGUY is a registered trademark of Advance Magazine Publishers Inc.

Portions of this book were previously published in *Details* magazine.

www.randomhouse.com/BB/

Library of Congress Card Number: 00-190234

ISBN 0-345-42727-0

Text design by H. Roberts Design
Cover design by David Stevenson
Cover illustration by Jean-Philippe Delhomme

Manufactured in the United States of America

BVG 01

to Fred Pressman
and Fred Hughes,
great style guys

The author extends his thanks to Fabien Baron, Michael Caruso, Gad Cohen, Art Cooper, Jean Phillipe Delhomme, Joe Dolce, Simon Doonan, Ariel Foxman, Heloise Goodman, Jean Paul Goude, Duncan Hannah, Brandon Holley, David Johansen, Tom Kalendarian, David Keeps, Anne Kennedy, Calvin Klein, Neil Kraft, Doug Lloyd, Hooman Majd, Wayne Maser, Richard Merkin, Chris Moore, Gina Nanni, Ronnie Cooke Newhouse, John Pearse, Bonnie Pressman, Gene Pressman, Phyllis Pressman, Peter Rizzo, Michael Skidmore, Debbie Smith, James Truman, Paula Greif Zanes, and Michael Zilkha.

Style and Guys

"A good plain look is my favorite look."
—Andy Warhol

S tyle isn't fashion. Fashion is about what everybody's doing, what everybody's wearing. Style is about what you're doing, what you're wearing. Fashion is about elitism and defining one's self in the social pecking order. Style is about expressing yourself, not a consensus. Style exists in the context of fashion, but its motives and its MO are the opposite of fashion. Fashion is avant-garde conformity. Style is individuality and growing as a person.

Style loves to be contrary. I want to set myself apart, not just from the crowd, but from myself, too. I want to be a contradiction. The world is in flux and I am, too. I want to reflect tradition and invention, ethnic diversity, multicultural dialogue, curiosity, and knowledge. Most of all, I want to look like my bad self. I want to look like a work in progress. I want to look like I'm alive, very alive.

Great style has always been about doing almost everything right and something, maybe just one thing, completely and inge-niously wrong. Be it a glitch, an oversight, or an improvisation, that's what makes for individualism. Imperfection that requires imagina-tion. Islamic carpet weavers always weave an imperfection into their patterns so the devil doesn't get into it. That's the idea behind making a mistake, or at least a transgression, in dressing, decorating the pad, even talking.

The great innovators in men's style have always been devil-may-care dudes who made mistakes, did it their own way, or took shortcuts that other people thought were so fab they imitated them. That's why today we have cuffs on our pants and nobody buttons the bottom button of their vest. But if you do button it, out of ignorance or rebellion, maybe that's style.

Today's goof is tomorrow's standard of excellence. The history of fashion is the history of mistakes, faux pas, glaring omissions, and utter disregard for the right way of doing it. The first time I met David Bowie he was wearing two different-colored socks. It could have looked stupid but it didn't. Maybe because he has two different-colored eyes.

When Jamaican-born Patrick Ewing, the star center of the Knicks, began playing ball for Georgetown in relatively frigid Washington, D.C., he was a prodigious perspirer and caught a cold, so he started wearing a T-shirt under his jersey to keep warm in February gyms. Pretty soon the look spread throughout the Big East Conference and then throughout college hoops. When Michael Jordan began playing for the Bulls he started wearing oversize shorts because he had his North Carolina shorts on underneath for good luck. It caught on so big-time that now some sports federations are trying to legislate against the frightening epidemic of baggy shorts.

Bottom line: The rules of fashion are made to be broken. Anybody can follow the codes and dress "properly." It takes imagination to dress in a way that challenges the status quo, recodes the nodes, and might even change the way the world wears things.

If you dress with taste and care, if you wear nice clothes and still leave something amiss, it shows that you know what you're doing and what you're not doing. You have confidence. You have *cojónes*, balls. You're not reporting directly to anyone stylewise. You're a free agent of taste. You're the boss, or you look like one anyway.

A personal note: I guess I have always been a stylish guy, even before I knew it. I think my parents and my grandparents gave me my start, but by the time I was six they wouldn't buy me anything without my approval. I loved to shop. My favorite foods were caviar, anchovies, and capers. My idea of a well-dressed guy was General MacArthur. When I was eleven my parents moved to New Jersey, and the first time we drove into New York I made them drive me to the Stork Club and wait for me outside. The maître d' was so impressed by this audacious act he took me around and introduced me to everyone.

By the time I reached puberty I had my look together. My big influences were my grandfather, who wore only white shirts for business; my grandmother, who said she'd never let her daughter go out with a guy in a pink shirt; Cary Grant; Gary Cooper; Arnold Palmer; and Dobie Gillis. It wasn't long before the hippie days and the youth revolution, and I was there, on the barricades, with over-the-shoulder hair, Jesus Christ beard, Brooks Brothers oxford cloth shirt, khakis, and Peal shoes. It might have been the end of the world, but I was determined to do it my way.

In the seventies I was wearing the same clothes, by this time well ripped, and I still believe it was me and not the Sex Pistols or Richard Hell that invented the ripped-clothes look. Looking back at the mid and late seventies, I see pictures of myself moving into a new synthesis of thrift-store elegance. Fortunately, I had gotten a job working at Andy Warhol's Factory, where we repioneered short hair in reaction to hippie cops and the Charles Manson look. It was there that I met one of my mentors, Frederick Hughes, who showed me that tradition could be the most avant-garde thing. Fred wore Savile Row suits, bespoke shoes, and bought us art deco costume jewelry from Paris, and he said things like "Men should wear black to show off the girls' dresses."

I also learned an enormous amount from another Fred, Fred Pressman, son of Barney Pressman who founded Barneys New

York. Fred was a truly great man, kind, elegant, and witty. He knew everything there was to know about men's clothing, the way it should be worn, and the way a man should comport himself. Like the English aristocrats who gave their suits to their valets to wear until the suits lost their crispness, Fred cultivated a certain lived-in look. His consummate elegance always had something a little off about it. His collar might be showing a tiny bit of wear because a good shirt was something you hated to let go of. But Fred wasn't a fuddy-duddy. I remember one day when I was working on Barneys advertising and Fred and I were looking over new men's samples, he picked up a long black overcoat from Jean Paul Gaultier. Fred must have been seventy at the time. He stared at the coat for a while and then said, "You know, if I were thirty years younger and four inches taller, I'd wear this."

With Fred Pressman, or Fred Hughes, or with my grand-father, it was never really about the clothes, although they loved the clothes; it was that the clothes reflected an attitude and a code, that of being a gentleman. Their clothes were only a token of a larger view. They dressed well out of respect to others and the world.

Guys and Girls

"All girls should have a poem written for them even if we have to turn this God-damn world upside down to do it."

—Richard Brautigan

"The goddesses that existed alongside the gods in primitive religions are in fact no longer within our emotional range," he thought. "Any relationship we might have to such superhuman women would be masochistic."

—Robert Musil, *The Man Without Qualities*

Some people think of style as what you're wearing, but style applies to every outward manifestation of your character and personality. The way you wear your hat and the way you sip your tea. Style is what you can't take away from me. Style is how we deal with the world, too. It's what happens when you have a unique personality that knows how to relate with other personalities.

Take girls, for example. Girls respond to style in a guy. Not just the way he looks, but the flair with which he treats her. The smoothness of his moves.

The first thing to remember about dealing with women is that we are different species. Different human races. And yet we are all one. Once you learn to keep these conundrums in mind, relations between the sexes get a lot easier. Women think very much like men. They have similar hopes and fears and fears and fears. A lot of the same things please them, like flattery, attention, consideration. A lot of the same things attract them, like indifference and unattainability.

But the most important thing to keep in mind in a relationship is the Golden Rule, do unto women as you would have them do unto you. Even though they are a different species, treat them with humanity and respect and you might get it back in return.

Men aren't from Mars and women aren't from Venus, but there are significant differences. A lot of men, for example, are dogs. They act exactly like dogs. It's all about sniffing, instinct, and having to be disciplined. Sheer dogness will get you somewhere with bitches, but it will get you nowhere with the ladies. If you are a dog, seek transcendence, my best friend. Practice virtue and humanity. Or fake it until it catches on.

Girls are attracted to blokes, bounders, and cads, but they always wind up going for gentlemen in the long run. (Maybe after a few divorces.)

An acquaintance I like and would almost consider a friend sometimes ignores me in social situations—large parties, for example. In small groups she is very friendly. What's up? Is she a snob?

There are two possible explanations: (1) Yes. (2) Maybe it's bad vision. I once thought someone a terrible snob because if I would see her across the room at parties, she would seem to ignore me, but at other times, in more intimate situations, she was warm. I found out she was incredibly nearsighted. You can always ask her if this is the case. If she isn't nearsighted, this is as good a way as any of letting her know her behavior is peculiar.

A girl I see a lot of is usually very late for dates. I hate sitting in a restaurant by myself for an hour. I've mentioned it many times. She's still late, but I don't want to dump her. What do I do?

I had a friend like yours, and I invented the twenty-minute rule, aka the Karen Rule. If she's more than twenty minutes late, she pays for dinner. And at about eighteen minutes after the appointed time, I start perusing the wine list for oddities.

I recently started dating a very liberated woman. I myself am old-fashioned, and I believe that I should pay for her on our dates. Should I let her pay for herself?

I think we all need to be flexible in these situations. When there's a significant gap in wealth or liquidity I always invoke the Fortensky Rule. The rich one pays for the expensive stuff, dinner, tropical vacations, champagne. The poor one pays for the newspaper, coffee, bowling, draft beer. Everybody gets to pay for something regularly. All you have to do is say, "I'll get this one." She'll say, "I'll get this one." Everyone will possess the dignity generosity affords, and the sex will probably improve.

Who pays on a blind date?

You do. The guy. Who did you think was going to pay? The person who set you up? It could be Dutch, but that idea would have to come from her.

If you're set up on a blind date and the person is unattractive, can you split before she figures out who you are?

Don't you hate yourself for even asking? This person might not be your life partner in waiting, but if you have a shred of humanity, she might turn out to be a pretty good friend. Somebody thought there was something there. Maybe you have Platonic potential.

How do you write a love letter? Is it a lost art?

Some people think the only way to write a love letter is in disappearing ink. I myself don't see any real reason to put it in writing. Maybe I'm cynical, but it seems like love letters usually wind up in the wrong hands or as Exhibit B. The love letter originated in a time without telephones, so the nature of it has changed. Now it is often used by people who don't have the nerve to express their true feelings verbally. The love letter is no substitute for nerve, men. If she's in Guam and you're in Lhasa, love letters can be very important. But if you're both near phones, think twice.

There is something to be said for the love fax. It gives you the same chance for premeditation that a letter allows, but with the immediacy of a phone call. Of course, it may fall into the wrong hands, but that's a good reason for romantic code names and the entertaining world of erotic euphemisms.

No matter how a date goes, I'm always uncomfortable when it's time to say good night. What do you say when you want to see her again? What do you say when you don't? What about the kiss?

If you want to see her again, just tell her sincerely how much you enjoyed yourself and that you'd like to do it again. If you don't want to see her again, just tell her insincerely how much you enjoyed yourself and leave it at that. As for the kiss, take your cue from her. If she presents her cheek, kiss her on the cheek. If she presents her lips, go for it. If she really likes you in that special way, it will be lips, sooner or later.

I've been dating a girl I really like. She wants me to meet her parents. I'm terrified. What should I wear? What should I bring? What should I say? What shouldn't I say?

Be yourself. They'll be seeing the real you eventually, so you might as well be real from the start. Just dress nicely and neatly in your own way and avoid wearing anything particularly frightening. A suit or sweater and slacks are bound to make a better impression than a studded motorcycle jacket and bondage pants. If you're invited for dinner, you might bring a nice bouquet of flowers—not roses, maybe tulips or lilies. It's safer than wine for a first meeting. You can't go wrong being complimentary of their daughter—they're bound to be proud of her. Just don't overstate your degree of intimacy with her. What shouldn't you talk about? The tattoo of their daughter's name you've got on your butt. Your HIV test. Your old girlfriend. Your sex life. Politics!

I was very close with my ex-girlfriend's parents. Now that we're not together, should I stay in touch with them?

You can always send them a Christmas/Hanukkah/Kwanzaa card. And you can leave it up to them. Chances are they have plenty of friends their own age. Let it go. There are plenty of other girls' parents out there.

I'm in love. I want to send flowers. Is this corny?

Corny? Corny can be charming. Go with your cornball instincts. Roses are the corniest and also very nice, but you might not want to send them until your relationship has progressed to a certain point, i.e., home plate.

I'm a big fan of sending something living. Even if she's a plant killer, it will last longer than roses, doesn't go through an unsightly wilt, and every time your beloved looks at it (or cares for it) she'll think of you. Orchids are great, although they can be pricey. Amaryllis or paperwhites are generally no more than a fancy dozen roses. You could go for some live tulips or a small hydrangea. Consult your better florists on something with some life span that's in season.

If you want to go with cut flowers, use the best florist you can find. Their flowers will be the freshest and last longer. Some flowers last a really long time. Cut orchids and lisianthus can last for weeks. Also consider fragrant flowers, which not only look good but fill the room with a delightful odor—freesia smells great. So do Casablanca lilies.

It takes an artist to create a good mixed bouquet and there aren't many artists out there, so it's usually best to go with a single type of flower in a single color. I'm a tulip guy myself—big white French tulips are very sexy. I always tell them to "hold the greens." Usually the greenery florists add don't do anything for the bouquet.

When you buy flowers for your own place, always trim the stem ends on an angle. Remove any foliage that would be under water. Use room-temperature water and always ask the florist for packs of Floralife or another cut-flower food that you add to the water to extend the life of the blooms. If you don't have flower food, a single aspirin added to the water will also help.

My apartment looks like Oscar Madison lives there. I'm a hopeless slob. How can I hope to entice a woman into this environment?

You could date the visually challenged, or you could change your life. I'd suggest the latter, because any good woman with at least one functional sensory system will find out sooner or later that your life is in disarray. If you hope to succeed with women, cultivate neatness. Neatness will not only make you more attractive, it will pay off in other ways. You will be able to find long-lost items. Basic physical organization will lead to basic mental organization. The quality of your work will improve. You'll earn more money. You'll score better chicks. Of course, you may be getting away with slovenly behavior now. You may think that this "cry for help" is appealing to a certain type of woman. Maybe she's picking up for you now. Fine, if you want to date the maid, but you'll pay for it later. Clean up your apartment and keep it that way. It doesn't have to be perfect, but your dirty laundry and dishes should not be visible. Dim lighting and candles will help a lot. Hot tip: dripless candles. And if you're hopeless, hire professionals to clean up your sty. Do you really want the kind of woman that will put up with your mess? Of course not.

Do you think it's okay for a man to ask a woman out to lunch or on a date if she is currently seeing someone else?

Lunch is a pretty safe bet. I don't think of lunch as a date. Maybe you're talking business. It's not okay to ask a woman out on a date if she is seeing someone else exclusively, but if you dislike the person she is seeing and think that she would be much better off dating you, then you might try it. The worst that could happen is that she'll suggest lunch.

I'm going to go out with a girl who lives in a doorman building. Do I kiss her good night outside or in the lobby? What if she doesn't ask me up?

If the mood is right and you think it's going to be more than a friendly peck, it should happen outside. A kiss on the cheek is about it once you're under the watchful eyes of the doorman. And if she doesn't ask you up, better luck next time.

I am dating an American Gladiator (female). The sex is out of this world, but the rest of the relationship is not what I need to be satisfied. I have had a few other offers and I'm finding it hard to say no. Should I leave my fifteen seconds of fame and find someone more compatible, or stick with it and see what happens?

Where will you ever find another girl who can beat you into submission with a pugil stick? That's something special you've got there, mister. I knew that American Gladiator ladies had to go out with somebody, but I always assumed it would be each other. The sex is great? Maybe you can find the other things you need to be satisfied from friendships. Besides, who knows if she's going to let you go? Maybe she can broaden her horizons. Look how she's broadened her body.

I have a girlfriend whose clothes I hate. What can I do?

You probably shouldn't tell her that you hate her clothes. You should let her know what you like in women's clothing. Admire an actress, admire a girl on the street, but express your taste. Maybe she'll take the hint. If she doesn't take the hint in a few months, you might consider dumping her. Beauty may be only skin deep, but taste is voluntary.

What music works for seduction?

Music works. It amplifies our charms, feeds our imaginations, and gives us rhythm if we need it. Good old D. H. Lawrence wrote, "Man must make love to music, and woman must be made love to, to a string and saxophone accompaniment. It is our inner necessity." Undoubtedly there are cases where Weezer or Mozart might work. But in the swinging adult world of the Style Guy, jazz reigns supreme. *Duke Ellington and John Coltrane, John Coltrane and Johnny*

Hartman, Miles Davis's *Kind of Blue*, Bill Evans's *Everybody Digs Bill Evans*, Kenny Burrell, various Sinatra, Billie Holiday, Sarah Vaughan, and Dinah Washington. There are guys who swear by Johnny Mathis. I swear by Ben Webster's *The Warm Moods*, *Chet Baker with Fifty Italian Strings*, and Kenny Burrell's *Midnight Blue*.

How do you break a date gracefully?

As soon as possible. It's not good to break the date after she has begun to get dressed for it. She may hate you for years. As soon as you know you have to, do it.

Break a date only out of necessity. A real man stands by his word and keeps his appointments. You'd better be contagious or genuinely sick, have a genuine emergency at work or an actual mission of mercy. Don't break a date because a better one came along. If the better date finds out you dumped the worse date, they'll both think you're a schmuck, which, by the way, you would be. Tell the truth. Don't fictively send your grandmother to the hospital again. It could come true. If you lie, you'll be found out. And, hey, you can always tape the game.

I'm a twenty-five-year-old grad student teaching an undergrad class. I have a crush on one of the sophomores in my class. I see her three times a week for an hour. I want to approach her and ask her to spend some time with me outside of class, but I'm not sure it's appropriate. What do you think?

What's really appropriate is that you wait until she isn't your student anymore. Then you won't have any power over her and can approach her in an uncomplicated way. Until then, just stay warm, friendly, and charming.

My girlfriend gave me a sweater for my birthday. I hate it. It's ugly.
Can I exchange it? Do I tell her?

You not only can, you should. Relationships are often ruined by
people holding back their ideas and feelings. Relationships can be
ruined by taste clashes, too. It's important for people to understand
one another's tastes, even though they don't have to share them.
Tell her you appreciate the gift but explain to her just what it is that
you don't like about it. Believe me, if you gave her something really
garish, she'd either bury it in the closet or exchange it.

There's a hot chick I work with and I think she's into me. The
problem is that she has a roommate and I still live with my par-
ents. How can I seal the deal without her knowing that I still live
with Mommy and Daddy?

I don't see any stigma about living with Mommy and Daddy,
assuming that you, dear reader, are well under thirty. Just inform
her of your domestic status, and if she is truly as interested as you
think she is, she will undoubtedly be able to determine when her
roommate will be elsewhere.

Whenever I meet a girl for the first time I usually do pretty well
conversationally, but I find it hard to keep it going as I try to build
a relationship with the girl. I don't consider myself shy. I'm not
afraid to talk, but I often find myself having nothing to say. It's
gotten to the point where girls are always saying, "Why are you so
quiet?" It's embarrassing. I'm not a "sweet talker." What are some
good topics of conversation for a romantic moment?

The best romances often begin as friendships. What do you talk
about with your friends? Try treating your dates as friends. Don't
think about where the relationship is going or what you want from
the girl, just go with the moment. Talk about art, music, politics,

fashion, food—you might even be able to talk to some women about sports. Just be yourself. And if you can't think of anything, you can always resort to the old standby—ask her about her life, about her childhood, about what she thinks. Chances are she will find this an endlessly interesting topic. As for "sweet talk," it's overrated. Phone sex talk is phony sex talk. Just keep it real and sincere and interested and you'll be respected.

I have a great girlfriend. She's beautiful and funny and we have a great time. The only problem is that sometimes she has BO. I don't want to hurt her feelings, but it's a real turnoff. What can I do?

Say "Let's take a shower." Showering together could save water and your relationship.

I'm a single guy. Sometimes when I sleep with a woman for the first time, I worry about passing gas while I'm asleep. What precautions can I take?

First, go see *Good Will Hunting*, then if you're still worried about nocturnal farting, try adding a few drops of Beano, (available in many health food stores and drugstores) to your food. This enzymatic product, designed for taking the sound effects out of legume-based dishes, can be added to many foods to cut down on your production of natural gas. But just remember, even dignified statesmen and top models fart, too.

Is it wrong to be attracted to my former stepsister? My dad used to be married to her mom. They were divorced a year ago. Is this incest?

No. Even if they were still together, it wouldn't be wrong to be attracted. It might be unwise to act on it, but attraction happens, kid. No, it's not incest. You may go for it if you like.

I recently introduced myself to my ex-girlfriend's father. We were both on the sidelines watching her in a sporting event. Now she's upset. Did I do something wrong?

No. Not this time, anyway.

My best friend is going out with a girl I liked first. I know he has herpes and maybe other STDs. Should I tell her? He won't. Or will that just look like sour grapes?

Why is this person your best friend? To be a friend you have to have some compassion and generosity. If he's the type who would put a girl at risk for his own pleasure, he doesn't have a shred of either. I think you should look for a new best friend. How do you know he wouldn't tell her? Ask him if he will. If he won't, you would be right to warn her. It won't necessarily make you look good in her eyes, but it's the right thing to do if you think they are intimate.

My ex has things in my apartment. My new significant other noticed them. Is the damage already done?

Assuming she knows that it's really over, the ex's belongings are just an unwanted reminder of her. Why do you still have her stuff? Ask her to pick it up, offer to deliver it, and if you don't get a response, put it in storage. Now.

Is it true that chocolate cures PMS?

Yes. But so do flowers, champagne, and expensive restaurants.

What are the limits on PDAs in movie theaters?

The good old-fashioned custom of holding hands would seem to be fine. A head on a shoulder is okay, if it doesn't block the view.

Anything else is better done elsewhere, like a motel room with a mirrored ceiling and a proactive bed. Remember Pee-wee Herman! In general I'm not a big fan of public displays of affection. It usually makes me want to yell, "Hey, rent a room!"

I'm meeting her parents for the first time in their home for dinner. Gift suggestion?

Flowers. One kind, not an arrangement. Spend at least as much as you'd have paid for the meal in a restaurant, including drinks, but not much more. No card, obviously, unless her parents are comedians.

Is it weird to ask for a date via E-mail?

Not really, unless you're too afraid to call and then it's a little nerdy.

Is it rude to break up over the phone?

The only proper way to end it is in person. You may have to deal with tears and a scene, but that's the price of freedom. The only exception is when you have a real long-distance relationship and aren't scheduled to see one another for weeks. Then you can do it over the phone if you have to, but it's a cowardly way to break up a local romance just out of fear of having a plate thrown at your head.

A girl I spend a lot of time with never introduces me to other people when they engage her in conversation and not me. Am I wrong to get upset? Should I just introduce myself?

She is being rude and not giving you your propers. Yes, introduce yourself, and she should get the point eventually. If she doesn't, tell her she's being rude. You may quote me.

What are classy, cheap venues for dates? I'm sick of the drinks-and-dinner scenario.

I'm a big fan of bowling as a date option. It's almost even more fun if you're not that good. Miniature golf is fun. Pool. Amusement parks. Canoeing. Games are good. Sporting events, especially something like baseball where the action is slow enough to allow for talking. Ballroom (as opposed to disco) dancing. Any situation where you can really talk. I think the movies are a bore as a date, especially early on, since you sit there for two hours not speaking to each other.

My girlfriend is always asking me if she looks fat. She does a little. What should I say?

Well, you could say, "Since you keep asking me if you look fat, you must feel fat. Maybe you should lose a few pounds." You might add that you find her fine the way she is, which isn't a big lie because you haven't dumped her over the avoirdupois. Or, hey, fuck it, tell her the truth.

Are oysters really an aphrodisiac?

Sure. So is really expensive black caviar, cashmere, a Porsche. So is money.

How do you pick a bottle of wine for the purposes of seduction?

Champagne—not just some sparkling white wine, but the genuine French article—is a traditional romantic cocktail. It will add an air of festivity to your lusty intentions. However, the idea of men plying resisting women with liquor and/or drugs is utterly vile and pathetic. Wine and champagne are nice for loosening up the mutually attracted, but anyone contemplating slipping the resistant object of their desire a Mickey, as in the use of Rohypnol, "the date-rape drug," is repulsive, and anyone who actually does it should enjoy his next romp in the slammer.

I want to get engaged and buy my girl a nice ring. All of the ads and TV commercials say that I should spend two months' salary. I don't want to be cheap, but this seems ridiculous to me. What is the real norm, and what should I look for?

This two-months'-salary bit is one of the most evil advertising campaigns ever conceived. It is designed to appeal to women, not men. Or it's supposed to make guys feel guilty and obliged to incur ridiculous debt. If you're going to get married, there are a whole lot of realistic expenses you're going to have to take care of. Would your fiancée rather have a pretentious ring or a nice car or a great honeymoon or a good apartment? An engagement ring is a token of your esteem. It's important, but it's still a token. What is really important is your love, not some symbol of it. You should buy a ring that you can really afford. And if you can't afford one now, it can always come later. The diamond miners would love nothing more than getting you to pay 20 percent interest on a useless piece of carbon. I think the best engagement rings are antiques. You can find some great pieces, mounted more beautifully than a new ring, for a considerably smaller investment.

Do engagement rings have to be diamonds to count?

No. But I wouldn't spring something else as a surprise. Some women prefer rubies, sapphires, or emeralds, but you'd better hear it from the fiancée's mouth before acting on it. Lady Di's famous engagement ring was a sapphire.

How can I get my girlfriend interested in sports? If she was into it, I'd have a lot more fun.

You can lead a girl to sports, but you can't make her watch. Today many women have developed an interest in sports because of Michael Jordan or Tiger Woods or Derek Jeter. If the physical thing doesn't get her, there's not much chance that the lore and tradition will. Forget it. Watch the game with the guys and let her do her thing, too.

How can I convince my girlfriend to wear spike heels? They really turn me on.

Confess your fetish and tell her if she doesn't start wearing them, you will.

How do you determine whether you're hanging out with someone or on a date?

Ask them if they want to fuck. If they do, chances are it's a date.

I've been dating somebody for a while and was wondering when it's okay to say "I love you."

As Kris Kristofferson wrote, "Freedom's just another word for nothing left to lose." What was the question?

Sex Guys

"I remember my first erections. I thought I had some terrible disease or something."

—Joe Brainard, *I Remember*

"Just because people love your mind doesn't mean they have to have your body too."

—Richard Brautigan

Guys are dogs. Guys are horny. It's the big disadvantage that we have in dealing with women. Women need it just as much as guys. Women enjoy it just as much as guys. But they're a lot cooler about it. The time frame works in their favor.

What guys have to always keep in mind is the cardinal rule of sex: Women always pick the guys. Women control consent. They own it. You can attract them, appeal to them, woo them, but when it comes to sex, women wear the pants.

I have been dating a girl for some time now. She seems to really like me and she kisses me, but she won't go to bed with me. How long should a guy wait?

No two cases are the same. But I asked Madonna this question once, and she said five dates, and she ought to know. But instead of asking me, maybe you should ask her: "How long should a guy wait?"

Who pays for birth control? I used to pay for condoms, but now my girlfriend is on the pill. Do I have to sponsor this new form of birth control?

If she asks, you could certainly pay half. All birth control involves two parties. It's not inappropriate for them to share the cost, no matter whom it works on. If you're a tight-type guy, you could always deduct half of your old condom expenses from your donations to her pill fund. By the way, don't construe this as Style Guy approving of birth control pills. If I were Style Gal, I wouldn't take 'em.

I'm having a problem with premature ejaculation lately. Do you know how to curb this problem? What causes it?

You could look at it this way: There is no such thing as premature ejaculation. There are only women who come too late. Your problem, my dear boy, is, perhaps, sex starvation. As soon as you begin having enough sex, you will ejaculate at precisely the right time. Have more sex. By any means necessary.

I'm twenty-two and since my teens I've had a problem with premature ejaculation. Usually after only two minutes of sex I have an orgasm. This is ruining my relationship. Is there any help for this problem?

Think of the millions of men buying Viagra to be able to do what you do so easily. You might try having sex more often. Lock yourself in the bathroom with your favorite porno magazine an hour before your next date and have a date with yourself. See if you don't last longer later. Or try a multiple-performance date. Maybe Act 2 will go better than Act 1. Some men try to mentally distract themselves during the act. In the ZZ Top song "Woke up with Wood," Billy Gibbons suggests thinking about basketball as a de-excitement technique. Also, most sex shops sell "delay" creams, which contain mild local anesthetics. I have no info on the performance of these preparations. Maybe some of our readers can fill me in. If none of this helps, see a doctor. They undoubtedly have something to slow you down.

I'm not sure how the self-described "conservative, old-style Style Guy" can quote ZZ Top lyrics with a straight face, much less their ridiculous suggestion that a man distract himself with basketball thoughts in an attempt to stave off the premature moment of truth. The last thing a poor soul with a hair trigger needs is a vision of hot, sweaty flesh bumping and grinding at breakneck pace, the ultimate object of which is to "score" by "taking it to the hole." Prolonging paradise requires a daydream of Victorian modesty, something that builds long, slow tension. Something more conservative and old style: baseball.

Style Guy is a personal friend of Billy Gibbons, who, despite his hair and beard, is in many ways a conservative, old-style guy himself. He's a blues guy, after all. Perhaps I forgot to mention that if the game of basketball itself isn't enough, you could always think specifically of Gheorghe Muresan, Shawn Bradley, or Larry Bird. And don't forget that baseball gave us the most common of scoring metaphors: getting to first base, second base, third base, and, of course, stealing home.

My fiancé is about fifteen years older than me, and he loses his erection during sex when he wears condoms. I've never encountered this before and don't know how to deal with it without threatening his manhood. Do you think he's just trying to get out of wearing condoms?

My guess is no. Everybody wants to have a good time. I'd suggest you try the new thinner condoms. This is one area where money is well spent, so buy the best, thinnest ones you can find. If that doesn't make a difference, there's always Viagra. From what I've heard, he could be wearing a wetsuit and still wouldn't lose his erection.

What is the right point in a relationship to get tested for HIV? What if the girl I'm dating gets freaked out?

The right point is before you do anything. Assuming that she's not a virgin, she shouldn't get freaked out about taking a test or you taking one. She should be reassured. Unless you've already had unprotected sex and have reason to worry.

I've read that circumcised men are 33 percent more likely to receive oral sex. I'm almost thirty. Would it be risky for me?

One of our editors eighty-sixed his foreskin at the age of twenty-three and describes the procedure as "practically a breeze." I don't remember losing mine, nor was I consulted, but the three distinct advantages of getting it done as a man are (1) you're expecting it, (2) you get anesthetized, and (3) you know what lies ahead may be more head.

It's true that I don't know what I'm missing. Anyway, there are several Web sites dealing with the pros and cons of foreskins, so set your search engines on circumcision, boys, before you call the mohel.

[After the previous answer appeared, a reader wrote that my answer on the adult circumcision question was flippant and based on aesthetics and alleged female preferences. Other readers who are not circumcised also wrote in heavily in favor of keeping that foreskin.]

I've always wanted to do a hard-core version of that sexy scene in **From Here to Eternity** *with my girlfriend on the beach. Are there any risks?*

Aside from arrest? Well, sand is for external use only, so you'd better be careful or your girlfriend might suddenly find you the abrasive sort.

I've heard that men who shave their pubic hair are more acceptable to women than men who don't. I'm apprehensive about shaving. What do you think?

I think that pubic hair is not only acceptable, it's preferable on the verge of mandatory. Some women might harbor cradle-robbing fantasies whereby pubic baldness is hot, but is that the kind of gal you're looking for?

You recently answered a letter about men shaving their pubic hair. I think you may have misunderstood the writer's question. I doubt that he was talking about shaving it all off. I'm a thirty-year-old married male. I shave my testicles and a bit off the side and trim what's left fairly short. My wife, who shaves everything, likes the trimmed look and thinks it's better for oral sex.

Yes, indeed! I didn't mean to mislead. Trim that shrub, by all means. Nobody wants a big shaggy monster in their pants. (By the way, I think you are probably shaving your scrotum, inside which are located the invariably hairless testicles.) What I was getting at, and I think that writer was, too, is the total shave, the prepubescent look. It's a little infantile for my taste. But *chacun à son goût*, as French kinks say. By the way, Style Guy is astounded by the enormous volume of responses to this question. The ladies out there seem definitely in favor of mowing the lawn neatly. However, having somehow visited a nude beach in the Caribbean, I would strongly resist the temptation toward topiary designs—hearts, spades, Nike swooshes, etc.

How do you break the news to someone that you have herpes?

This is one of those bits of information that should be made available, as they say in the intelligence community, "on a need-to-know basis." Your mother doesn't really need to know.

Who does need to know is anyone you have sex with, and they should know before the fact. How to tell them: "I have herpes." Don't beat around the bush and tell them that you have a terrible secret. It's not so terrible. You could have a lot worse. Maybe they have herpes, too. The same, of course, goes true for any other sexually transmitted diseases you might carry. You'd appreciate your partner doing the same.

After a hot, sticky session I suggested to my partner that instead of sleeping on the wet spot we change the sheets. She was offended by my offer. What should a clean guy do?

I can understand that it might dampen the afterglow to immediately remake the bed. And, if you're real tidy, you might be disinclined to schmutz it up again. So I'd suggest that you throw a towel over the spot and make the change in the morning. A terry cloth bath towel might be obtrusive; how about a linen hand towel?

I share a three-bedroom apartment with two other guys. I have a great girlfriend. The only problem is that she's very vocal when it comes to lovemaking. How can I get her to lower the volume without lowering the passion?

What's her living situation? Does she have roommates? If not, maybe you should make her place your love pad. If she does have roommates, is she as vocal in her own place? Maybe you should try the loud, live phone-sex thing at her place and see how she likes it. Of course, if she's truly a great girl who gets carried away, I'm sure it's okay to tell her that you consider your lovemaking private and don't like the idea that there's an audience, that it takes away from your intimacy. If that doesn't work, ask her if she'd like to try one of those ball gags that they sell in the bondage department of sex shops. You never know.

A lesbian couple of my acquaintance would like me to be a sperm donor for their "baster" baby. What is the etiquette of that?

There is no etiquette where ethics are the issue. Would you, personally, like to have emanated from a baster and into their universe? If you're sure that's a yes and want children at a distance, go for it. Otherwise, get that new book on eunuchs and have it with you the next time you see them, and tell them you need a little more time to think about it.

I'm dating a woman who is very prim, and I think we are going to have sex soon. What is the most proper way of disposing with a condom after sex?

The best thing to do is scrunch it up in a tissue and dispose of it in a proper garbage can. Flushing them is safe sex but unsafe plumbing. Not a good idea. They should also be disposed of in a covered can, especially if pets are around. There's nothing Fido would rather chew on than a full lambskin condom, unless it's a funky tampon.

I work a lot of late nights with a beautiful woman. Sometimes when we are alone I feel a vibe between us. What is your opinion of sex in the office?

Sex in the office is not a good idea, unless you're in the "sex industry." Sex with a coworker can be the beginning of a beautiful relationship, but it is fraught with peril. Proceed cautiously. If you think there's a good chance of a mutual attraction, why don't you invite her out for a drink after work. If she says no, the vibe is probably coming from the fluorescent lights.

I'm usually up on what's hip, but lately some of my younger friends have been wearing bondage pants, chains, rings, and bracelets. What's bondage, and what does its paraphernalia signify?

Bondage pants are for playing the game "prisoners and jailers." Or for pretending that you are veal. Don't worry, these pants, too, shall pass.

What is statutory rape? What are the age limitations? Does it vary from state to state?

Statutory rape means having sex with someone under the age of consent. They can even be the aggressor, but if they're too young, they are jailbait. The age of consent does vary from state to state. Consult the handy table on page 941.

I have what is termed a hooded penis, so I cannot retract my fore-skin during erection. What can I do to make sex more enjoyable and less uncomfortable besides a circumcision?

See a doctor. Then see another doctor. It's always good to get a second opinion. Then you should probably get a circumcision. You'll enjoy sex more and so, probably, will your collaborators. I'm no doctor, but I don't believe this procedure involves serious, enduring pain. But I'd get a Polaroid of it before they cut. Then you can have before-and-after show-and-tell.

What is the best thing you can say to someone when you've prematurely ejaculated?

"Wow, I can't wait to do that again." Or "You are so exciting I just can't contain myself." Personally I don't think there is such a thing as premature ejaculation, as long as you have already removed your trousers. Certain feminists will argue that any ejaculation that occurs before the woman has experienced multiple orgasms is premature. Tell them they're ejaculating postmaturely. Don't worry. Chances are with a little practice and partnership you'll be ejaculating maturely in no time.

I hesitate to take showers in a public shower or locker room because I tend to pop a boner by surprise. I'm not gay but my erections are out of control. What should I do?

Think about Leonardo DiCaprio. If you don't lose your erection, you are gay. Try turning off the hot water.

Is it improper to leave nudie magazines on my coffee table?

If no one enters your home, it's no problem at all. But nudie magazines are not coffee table books, they're stroke books. I think they belong in your shirt drawer or under the mattress. If that seems tawdry, you could always have them bound in fine leather and keep them in the bookcase.

What's the appropriate tip on a ten-dollar lap dance?

My tip is, wear Depends instead of underwear.

Fashion Guys

"I have never felt the necessity of being with it. I'm all for staying in my place."

—Noël Coward

Fashion is for girls. I love watching it. I'd rather check out the babes in *Vogue* than in *Playboy*. I love watching some stylish statement suddenly appear on the girls on the street and then spread through the fashion-editor elite and into the magazines.

Fashion is for boys, too, all the young dudes. I pay attention to it, but I'll never become a fashion victim, because I don't like the game. Maybe it's because I have arrived at my manly prime, but I'm now more into a kind of classic thing. I feel like my suits should last as long as I do.

Men's fashion, like women's, is based on the great American marketing principle, planned obsolescence. I'm not buying into it. Suits come with buttons. These are to keep the jacket closed. A single-breasted jacket might have one, two, three, or four of them doing this important job. A double-breasted jacket might have four, six, or even eight. This is one of the key areas where a perfectly serviceable garment might become old looking. But the hell with it. I'm sticking with the classics, and if somebody doesn't like it, I can deal. If you look at Cary Grant's suits from the thirties, forties, and fifties, they still look good today. That's style, not fashion.

But don't get me wrong, guys. Youth is a time for experiment and change. You try on clothes like you try on who you are. It's okay to change, it's okay to make mistakes. But if you go in for fashion, go in for a look that suits you. You don't want to be a wanna-be. Start your own trend. Uniforms are okay for jobs that call for them. But the best look is one that has you written all over it.

I thought street fashion was about creativity, liberty, and some-times rebelliousness. Then how come there are these nonintuitive rules like never wear socks with sandals or never wear tight cutoff jeans? By making rules, how can fashion reach a pluralistic and truly democratic status? Isn't it time to end the hypocrisy and oppression of stylists?

Right on, my brother hippie man, there are no rules. True style is always creative. There are laws, though (in my town you'd better wear a shirt on Main Street or you'll get a ticket). There are, of course, corporate dress codes. There are invitations that make dressing suggestions, like black-tie or semiformal. There are signs that say NO SHIRT, NO SHOES, NO SERVICE. And there are principles and there are aesthetics. In fashion questions here, I'm basically dealing with aesthetics and advising men on making their way through a complex and often hostile work environment.

Nothing is cooler than seeing someone flaunting the so-called rules with great style. It's all personal. I never wear red. I'll wear a striped suit, striped shirt, and striped tie. I'll wear white socks, sure that they'll invite scorn, but it's because I believe and I care more about what I think than what they think. (Not to mention that I'm self-employed.) But you're right. Style is an art, not a science. Be true to yourself and look great by any means necessary. Allen Ginsberg could certainly carry off the sandals with socks and as for tight cutoff jeans . . . well . . . you're right, Fabio, just do it.

I wear glasses. Is it snobbish to have more than one pair to combine with different outfits and/or moods?

Heavens no, my dear boy! Every glasses wearer should have options. I destroy or lose at least two pairs of glasses a year, so I always have spares handy and they're always different. I always have a tortoiseshell pair, a black pair, and a metal pair. My titanium frames are virtually indestructible and actually survived being run over by a truck. Relax! Consume! Enjoy!

My girlfriend is a member of the work force, but I'm still a student. I want to look good when I go out with my girlfriend's coworkers, but I don't have much cash for clothes. Any ideas?

One good stylish outfit will go a long way, especially if it's simple and classic, like a black or navy suit with a white shirt. Or a black suit with a black shirt. You can wear it over and over again, and people will think of it as your trademark, not poverty. It worked for Johnny Cash. It can work for you.

I'm on a tight budget, but I need clothes to go out. What do you suggest for an inexpensive nightclub look?

I'll say it again. Black. It's groovy. It's sleek. It's harder to tell if it's expensive or basic. It doesn't show the dirt. If you have a hole in it, just wear something black underneath.

I'm a girl in her late twenties. Sometimes I like to wear my boyfriend's clothes—a sweater or an overcoat—whenever I stay with him on weekends. Lately he has started to reciprocate by wearing some of my stuff. Not underwear or anything kinky, but I still think it's socially unacceptable. Should I say something?

Yes, but don't be brutal about it. He got the idea from you. Maybe he was going for a Kurt Cobain kind of thing. Just tell him that your stuff doesn't suit him, and maybe you should lay off his stuff for a while.

Is it fashionably sound to wear a crewneck sweater with a polo shirt collar sticking out?

Certainly. Out, yes; up, no.

Is fur too effeminate for a heterosexual guy like me to wear on a coat?

Whether or not you are antifur—and I'm against trapped fur—men look stupid in fur coats. Fur collars don't look as stupid, and sometimes fur trim looks cool on the hood of a parka. I don't think fur brings much to your look, and if it came from a trapped, tortured animal that tried to chew its leg off in a trap, well, then it's a sin.

In the summer I wear shorts a lot and my supercool Vans, old school-style black with white stripes down the sides. Should I wear ankle-high socks or regular-length athletic socks bunched up around the ankle?

What do you like? Regular length sounds good to me. Personally I find one of the worst looks on men to be those little shorty socks designed for that sockless look that many golfers wear these days. They might give you a better tan, but for my money they look a little fruity. If you're going to wear socks, wear socks. Not Peds.

Say you're at a party having a good time and you turn around and see another guest wearing the same jacket you are.

You could compliment him on his taste. Or ask him if he's talked to Mom lately.

I'm an avid golfer. I notice that most professional golfers wear belts with metal tips on the end. I'm going to join a country club this year. Should I invest in metal-tipped belts?

You've got sharp eyes, mister. I have never noticed this phenomenon. I have noticed that slacks that have a matching belt made of the same fabric often have the metal belt tip of which you speak. This is to keep the fabric from fraying. There's no good reason, other than superfluous decoration, for a metal tip on a leather belt. I don't think it's an issue. No one has ever looked at me askance at my club, and my belts are not metal-tipped. It's just one less place to get hit by lightning.

I'm overweight. I'm making an effort and I'm losing weight, but in the meantime how can I dress to de-emphasize my bulk?

Wear dark colors. Stick with single-breasted jackets. Clothing with patterns should be avoided like ice cream, although subtle vertical stripes can help. Don't wear a huge loud tie. Don't wear spread collars. Stay away from jeans and, do I have to mention this, spandex.

My idea of cool is wearing 501xx 1955-model jeans, Doc Martens, and a white T-shirt. No jewelry. I'm twenty-one and I feel cool. Am I? I have shoulder-length straight hair.

If you feel cool, that's cool.

I was disturbed to read the letter from the girl who thinks she speaks for women when she says they hate men in jeans shorts. You agreed. I'm a good-looking guy. I get dates. But I wear jeans shorts all the time. Why should I renounce them? If the answer is good enough, I promise to turn myself in to the local fashion police. P.S. I always wear them knee length.

I'm not suggesting you renounce them. They're not Satan, son. I'm suggesting maybe you shouldn't wear them anymore. Just because you get dates doesn't mean you look good in your cutoffs. I don't think the ladies like them, generally speaking, usually because they are butt-hugging, cheek-showing, go-go boy gear. But, I suppose, some gals go for that Chippendales look. However, if your cutoffs are long enough and loose enough, you might not be disgracing yourself, like you would in, say, cutoff overalls or stretch jeans. Still, I don't think you can beat a good pair of casual Bermudas for airing out your legs.

I get confused by all the styles of glasses that are available. Are there any rules about specs and shades?

The only rule is, don't follow fashion when it comes to your face. Fashions will change, your face won't. Right now, small lenses are in fashion. If you have a big face, these will make it look even bigger. Why not take a tasteful friend with you for a second opinion when you go to the optician? They'll be more objective than the salesperson, and then later if you hate what you bought, you can always blame them.

I liked the old Sex Pistols punk style. Is it still cool to wear safety pins decoratively?

You bet your life! Safety pins will always be in style. They remind us to practice safe sex and drive safely, and they come in handy if you rip something. The safety pin was patented by Walter Hunt in New York City on April 10, 1849, making it like an Aries, dude. However, pins similar to safety pins have been found in the ruins of Celtic settlements dating from the third century. The safety pin came into widespread fashion use in the late 1970s, both as a clothing accessory and as a body fetish. British punks claim to have invented its use as an accessory. New York prototype punk Richard Hell also claims credit. But photographs exist showing Andy Warhol wearing safety pins on his black leather jacket in 1967. Perhaps this was picked up from window dressers who often wear multiple safety pins on a large safety pin when they are dressing dummies in store windows.

What's a smoking jacket?

It's a buttonless jacket resembling a double-breasted tuxedo jacket made of velvet, silk, or other luxurious materials. The collar is usually satin or velvet, and the jacket is usually closed with a sash. The smoking jacket is usually worn by a host, entertaining at home. Despite the name, it is still legal in the state of California.

I've been considering leather pants. Am I an idiot?

Possibly. But if you also buy a motorcycle, at least you'll have an excuse.

How should a vest be worn? I've seen many people wear them wrong, but I don't know what's right. Can they be altered?

Wearing them wrong? Well, the Ed Norton look (of The Honeymooners, not Larry Flynt), vest with T-shirt, does give off a sanitation-worker-type vibe. A vest looks best as a part of a matching suit or as a contrast to a blazer—a tartan vest can look great under a navy blazer, for example. I think a vest looks best with a shirt and tie. A vest over a turtleneck looks like a mismatch to me.

Usually a vest doesn't need to be altered because the belt in the back adjusts the fit. If it's part of a three-piece suit, it should fit if the rest of the suit fits. The main problem you see is vests that are too short, exposing shirt and tie. Usually this means the suit is too small; try a larger size. (Or maybe a long size.) The vest should be long enough to cover your belt buckle. The bottom button of a vest is usually worn unbuttoned. It's an old custom dating back to a fatso British royal, but it looks cool, so why fight it?

I'm thinking of wearing a suit jacket, a pair of nice Wranglers, and cowboy boots to a wedding. Is this appropriate?

If it's a cowboy wedding, yup.

I'm thinking of getting a tattoo. Any advice?

Think twice. I know it's almost a rite of passage these days. Everybody's doing it, unlike twenty years ago when it was kind of a jailhouse, bodybuilder, biker kind of thang. Now every model's got one. But just remember, it's permanent. If I were going to get permanently marked, I think I'd go for something abstract, like those black bars Henry Rollins has on his arms. Maybe a sun or a moon or one of those Celtic designs. I can't think of anything I'd want written on me for the rest of my life, although I have friends with tattoos in Chinese and Japanese that look pretty cool, and even though they mean something you don't exactly read it every time you see it. Tattooing a name on yourself isn't such a great idea; ask Johnny Depp, owner of "Winona Forever," or model Jaime Richard who wore the name Anthony for the Red Hot Chili Pepper several men ago. Things change even though they seem permanent, but tattoos don't. *Mom* is kind of sweet and traditional, and as Harold Melvin and the Blue Notes sang, "You only get one, you only get one." If you've gotta do it, my advice is go abstract and put it somewhere other than your face, neck, hands, or forearms.

I work as a PR manager, and I hate the dress-down attitude that's taking over. I dress up every day with a modern approach—flat-front pants, square-toe shoes, some shiny fabrics, body-hugging shirts. My girlfriend loves it. So do most women. Am I out of line?

No, my boy, you are at the head of the line! You have a great career in public relations ahead of you.

I shaved my head a month ago. Now it's growing back. Should I let it grow or shave it again?

Having never met you, I asked the Magic 8 Ball, and it said, "Don't count on it."

Is it appropriate to use large words if they are a natural part of your lexicon? If so, when?

Yup. Usually.

I have been searching to the answer to this for years. No one has an answer. Where did the expression dressed to the nines *originate and why?*

This expressions seems to be entirely obscure in origin. *A Dictionary of Slang and Unconventional English*, by Eric Partridge (Macmillan, 1961), finds its first use in Thomas Hardy in 1879: "dressed up to the nines." It is theorized that *the nines* was an expression of perfection, derived from nine being considered generally "the top" in numerology, also accounting for the expression *the whole nine yards*. *The Dictionary of Clichés* (Ballantine, 1987) cites an 1836 use: "praisin' a man's farm to the nines." Of course, *nines* also rhymes with *vines*, which is what natty players called their threads back in the day. It also rhymes with *fine wines*, and *Gregory Hines*. And let's face it, dressed to the eights doesn't sound as great.

What's your opinion on overalls for men? Is it for more than construction workers and farmers now? Is it fashion?

Overalls are certainly worn as fashion these days. My opinion is that they solve the tucking-in problem and fight plumber's butt for guys who are overweight. But then I never much liked the show-us-your-underwear look either.

I usually have to carry a few things with me—i.e., sunglasses, a notepad, a pocket camera—and I usually put them in the breast pocket of my shirt. They often fall out if I bend over, and I don't like that bulky effect. I usually take a jacket with me, even in the summer, so I have a place for my stuff. I feel too old for a backpack, don't need all the room of a shoulder bag or briefcase, and I'm very anti-fanny pack. What's the solution?

I'm with you on often wearing (or even just carrying) a jacket on summer days. And it sometimes comes in handy with extreme air conditioning. Backpacks are for the great outdoors, not urban areas. I hate getting slugged with them by people turning around. Hate those fanny packs, too; they make you look like a fanny. Male purses work only if you're wearing a full kilt ensemble. But there are slim briefcases. And you can find good sport shirts with flap pockets that button—from the world of designers to the world of army surplus. These will keep your shades and your pad in place when it's too hot for a jacket.

In the old days you could tell an artist by his beret, smock, sandals, and goatee. What's the postmodern equivalent?

Pants and shoes splattered with paint. Every painter wears jeans to paint in, and they tend to favor sturdy black leather shoes. Therefore if you want to affect an artist look, you need worn jeans with just the right paint-splash effect and shoes to match. Recently Helmut Lang sold perfectly passable painters jeans, but poseur shoes have yet to be marketed. Get some Doc Martens and buy some gesso, stand across the room, and splash them. Buy some foreign cigarettes, a boat-neck sweater, and you're almost ready for a one-man show.

Occasionally I sport a yellow vinyl jacket, a red turtleneck, and blue jeans. I'm from New York City, but now I live upstate and people can't accept it. Am I wrong or are they?

What do you mean they can't accept it? Do you get hoots on the street? Do they wave you out of their convenience stores? Keep wearing what you like. It's good for them. But if you switch to an orange vinyl jacket, they'll probably think you go to Syracuse and shut up. Vinyl is not *my* favorite fabric, but you like it, that's the important thing.

Why do lawyers and investment bankers wear suspenders?

To hold their pants up?

Why does everything have epaulets on it these days?

So at parties we can sing along with the Village People to "In the Navy"? So a perfectly good, well-made jacket will look embarrassing next year so you have to buy a new one and stimulate the economy? So you can stick your gloves under them when you go to the bathroom? So in case of a military coup, you'll be halfway there? I don't know. I just looked in my closet and couldn't find a single epaulet. Whew!

I like the idea of wearing a kilt. I'm straight and I'm not a drag queen, but I dig the look. Am I nuts?

No. Kilts are cool, but they're not for everyone and they're not for all occasions. To wear a kilt, I believe, one should have a Celtic heritage, unlike the German heir to the British throne who is often photographed kilted. Kilts are made of tartan plaid fabrics, and to wear such a tartan, you should belong to the family it represents or be prepared to defend yourself. And remember, kilts are to be worn without Calvins the way they were ten centuries ago, laddy.

I'm an initiate Goth. Have any tips for applying black eyeliner?

You must be a novitiate Goth. Ask your mother; she can explain it better than I can. I guess they tell you that at the initiation.

Recently I noticed a guy at work who wears nail polish on his thumbs. I didn't think much of it, but recently I've seen more guys on TV and in life that wear nail polish on their thumbs. Is this a new style? Is it cool?

I first saw this look on Penn Jillette, the corpulent, loquacious, self-enchanted member of the magic team Penn and Teller. I assumed that this was to indicate that although Mr. Jillette wears conservative clothing, he is not a normal person, or to give him something to talk about that would seem to be superfluous. Is it cool? No. Unless you're a big fat loud magician.

I've seen guys with one long fingernail on the pinkie finger. What's that about?

There are several explanations, none of them mutually exclusive. The first explanation I heard was that it was a sexual thing, something you might see on a pimp, the pinkie being the designated clitoral stimulator. A more likely explanation is built-in coke spoon. An even more likely explanation, related to women's long nails, is that it's an ancient way of showing that you don't labor for a living.

I'm into the Patagonia look. My girlfriend hates it, but I think it's cool. Who's right?

It depends. If you're planning to spend a lot of time in Patagonia—that is, the southern part of Argentina—it might be perfectly appropriate. This region of deserts and Andean mountains is rugged and wild. The name Patagonia goes back to the Portuguese explorer Ferdinand Magellan, who first explored the coasts of the area. He thought that the bushy-haired natives, dressed in fur, resembled the Patagon, a fabled monster. If you want to look like a fabled monster, which many people apparently do, since even Prada is mimicking this mountain-climbing outback look, then you're fine. But I myself don't see the relevance to polite, urbane society.

I was rather surprised to read your declaration that nail polish on guys is not cool, considering that the very magazine you write for has been promoting the look for the past few seasons. As far as nail polish being reserved for "big fat loud musicians" goes, you can find several cool musicians, artists, and one very cool director sporting the look in the pages of Details. *I don't see the encouragement of traditional, stereotypical, and conservative images when it comes to men's fashion as a positive thing.*

First of all I wrote "big fat loud magicians," not musicians. Everyone knows that rock musicians are allowed to wear nail polish and makeup. It might not work for investment bankers, but if you're in show biz, baby, anything goes. Secondly, I'm not a fashion adviser. It's Style Guy. Style isn't fashion, although fashion is a part of style. Fashions come and go, but style comes from within; it's a manifestation of your personality. I myself dress in a conservative context, but I'm pretty wild within that context. But I can still appreciate wilder styles than my own, whether it's Prince, Henry Rollins, the Beastie Boys, or Beck. I think everybody's style should be a manifestation of their creativity. I just don't dig nail polish. Even on women. And clear polish makes you look like a pimp.

I think that nail polish looks great on guys, but only black polish, and more guys should wear it, especially the younger ones. I have read in several articles that it is becoming more common for guys to wear nail polish. More hard-core band members are wearing it. I can see how it might look dumb on Penn Jillette, but on Matt Damon, Leo DiCaprio, or the Backstreet Boys it would be cool. How can you judge nail polish by some fat pig wearing it?

Now calm down. We're not reading carefully here. I was talking about this one-nail bit. If young guys want to wear black nail polish or rings in their eyebrows, I'm the last person in the world that's going to criticize them for it. I don't like the look, but who cares. The first guy I ever saw in black nail polish was Lou Reed back in the seventies. I thought he had slammed his hand in a car door. It's a look. It's probably a better look than clear polish, which is a sort of Atlantic City $5 blackjack dealer look.

Working Guys

"Work is a form of nervousness."

—Robert Benchley

S tyle is about expressing yourself, but there's always a context. For most of us our jobs and careers provide a lot of that context. Our work involves certain codes and conventions, and hopefully it involves a certain ethical standard. And, if we're lucky, it gives us a chance to be creative. Having a successful career usually means striking a perfect balance between the standards of your field and your own intelligence. Real success means giving something to your work that wasn't there before.

It's funny how company dress codes work. I once spent two weeks consulting at a large advertising agency. The first day I arrived dressed in a suit and tie. I like ties. The creative directors were dressed in shredded jeans, gym shorts, flip-flops, and Anthrax and Butthole Surfers T-shirts. The second day, someone took me aside and said, "You know, you don't have to wear a suit and tie." Yeah, I know. But I was just being me. Creativity comes in many forms. By looking like an account guy (well, actually a lot better than an account guy), I was a rebel in the creative department. Nice to shake 'em up once in a while.

Is it true you should always wear a suit (not a sport jacket and dress pants) to a job interview?

If you would be wearing a suit on the job, by all means. The strategy for most job interviews is to dress like you've already got the job. (This obviously doesn't apply for police, surgeons, deep-sea divers, etc.) If you're interviewing for a job as a fry cook or gas station attendant, a suit is optional. It's always good to look your best, and neatness definitely counts.

My boss just asked me out to dinner. I can't tell if she's flirting with me or not. Should I go? I'm kind of interested, but I don't know whether it's her or her authority that interests me. Who pays?

Go. So far it's a business dinner. By dessert you should know if she's flirting or not. Later you can take it or leave it. Yes, power can be sexy. That's okay. And she invited you, so she pays or the company pays.

My immediate superior takes credit for most of my best ideas. How can I let the big boss know what I've been up to without ruffling anyone's feathers?

There's probably nothing you can do that won't ruffle. But if you can manage to spend some time with the big boss, maybe he'll start to realize that you have a lot of good ideas and maybe he'll put two and two together. Don't try to discredit your superior. Maybe he'll do that all by himself. Such behavior is endemic to the corporate world. Big bosses are often able to see through it. You might pipe up and say, "Brilliant, sir! I wish I'd thought of that myself!"

I am switching jobs from a dress-up Madison Avenue firm to a casual Internet firm where the dress code is geared toward Star Trek. Do I wear my double-breasted suit and tie or play ball and dress down? What's an Internet account exec to do?

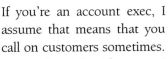

If you're an account exec, I assume that means that you call on customers sometimes. You might stick with your suits on days where you're outside the office. (Maybe you go a little more futuristic on ties. How about a Jerry Garcia tie?) Then on days when you have no outside work you can always go with the flow around the office and wear a Ferengi jumpsuit or a Vulcan caftan.

I'm a corporate lawyer in New York. I'm moving to L.A. to work for an entertainment law firm. Do I need a new wardrobe?

New York and L.A. culture have lots in common, but there are differences. And, of course, the climates are radically different. You'll probably need more summer or tropical-weight suits. You may also find your new environment a little more casual and/or fashion forward. But check out your peers in the new office before making a huge investment. My principal observation on the difference between New York and L.A. is that what's black in New York is white in L.A. and vice versa.

I'm in the market for a briefcase. I don't know whether to get a hard case or a soft one with a shoulder strap. What's better?

It depends on what you're going to use it for. I have an old beat-up soft leather one and a new, handsome hard leather one. The good thing about the hard one is that it will safely accommodate my laptop, plus papers, pens, and all. I still use the soft one when I just want to carry some papers. The advantage of the soft one is that it's light and takes up a little less space (under a plane seat or whatever). By the way, shoulder straps on a briefcase are a little New Age for my taste, but if you're comfy with it, okeydokey.

I work in a fairly conservative firm. Costume suggestions for a Halloween party?

Excellent Bill Clinton masks are available. Or why not go as Barney the purple dinosaur? Vampire teeth? A Rush Limbaugh tie? A Lieutenant Worf mask? Press-on nails and lipstick? If it's really conservative, maybe you should just wear women's underwear and not tell anyone.

What do you think of casual Fridays?

Communist plot? Maybe. Actually it would seem to be a part of a pseudoleveling of the workplace that coincides with the redefinition of white collar and blue collar. Casual Friday isn't really about Friday. It's creeping into Thursday. It's blurring the line between management and labor.

Casual isn't a bad idea. It's the spirit of the modern world. Workplaces have become more casual. It used to be "Yes, Mr. Doe." Today it's "Yes, John." We have become more egalitarian. On the face of it. But not in the heart of it. Once, the labor force was divided into obvious hierarchical structures, into the white-collar and blue-collar areas. White collar was cerebral, management, upper

and upper middle class. Blue collar was casual, physical, laboring—
lower and lower middle class. But today we've gone populist and virtual, and the distinctions have blurred. Nobody loves to wear a suit
more than a hard hat, and nobody loves to wear a hard hat more
than a suit.

Office dress codes have eroded visibly over the last twenty
years. In the early eighties guys in conservative suits, white shirts,
and conservative ties were fixing typewriters while guys in Italian
suits, colored shirts, wild ties, and porno suspenders were bor-
rowing billions from guys in Day-Glo tennis outfits. The old world
is dead.

The central office has given way to networks of remote PC
units. Your man in Maui might be wearing a thong, but if the num-
bers are there, he's solid. The root of the word *casual* is the Latin
casualis meaning chance. Today the circumstances of life and our
way of business is much more chancy, therefore more casual. The
tie and wing collar represented a belief in the judgment of God and
his angels. The high tops, sweats, and team jacket of today's creative director exec represent a belief that life is a jump ball, up for
grabs.

Still, casual is extremely codified and tactical. It's just as
formal as formal, with even more room for error, since there are no
blatant rules. And some people think that's scary, since they now
have to wear clothing and not a uniform. So now you have an
excuse to dress like yourself, not who you want to be. And that's
good. Huh? As long as you know who you are. So, who are you?
Are you casual? Are you willing to take a chance?

Guys in Suits

"Current millennia impulses tend toward disintegration, in style as in politics; but men's suits are neither post-modern nor minimalist, multicultural nor confessional; they are relentlessly modern, in the best classic sense."

—Anne Hollander, *Sex and Suits*

(Having asked Harold French which tailor made his suit.) "He should be humanely put down."

—Noël Coward

Suit—a synonym for a certain kind of guy. A functionary, a drone, an unoriginal person. But that's what happens when the clothes wear the man. If you wear the clothes and make them your own, if you transcend the idea of the uniform, then a suit can be your friend. A great suit is the ultimate weapon in a man's wardrobe.

I've been digging the revival of three-button sport and suit jackets, but I'm getting mixed signals on whether to button the top button or not. My tailor says no. Darren on **Bewitched** *and Ross Geller on* **Friends** *say yes. Who's right? And are three-button suits a fading fad?*

There are two kinds of three-button suits—a high-roll lapel and a low-roll lapel. Brooks Brothers suits and other traditional low-rolled three-button models show more shirt and probably look better with only the middle button closed. A high-rolled lapel, such as you might find on a Gucci or more fashion-forward suit, looks better with the top two buttons buttoned. Only Pee-wee Herman–type cats button the bottom button; it's a bit twee, as they say in the Isles of Britain. A lot of fashionables button only the top button, and that's okay if it looks good on you. And, no, three buttons are here to stay. I have a long body and not so long legs, and the best look for me is a high-rolled three, showing less shirt and tie. If you're a leggy dude, you might prefer a low-rolled three or a two-button. Two-button is big fashion on the runways these days. Can the one-button Vegas look be far behind?

Have movies such as Pulp Fiction and Men in Black rendered the single-breasted jacket kitsch, or are they more in fashion than ever?

Than ever. Neither single nor double will ever constitute kitsch alone. It is extremist proportions (such as tiny or massive lapels) and fashion-victim details (epaulets, anyone?) that do that job. The most kitsch thing about single-breasted is that politicians always wear them, so avoid the white shirt and red tie.

How does one wear a four-button single-breasted suit? Or, for that matter, does one? I'm going shopping with my style-conscious wife and want something different.

Four-button is a fashion statement. It may not be an enduring state-ment, but these suits can look good on tall, slim guys. Usually they have fairly narrow lapels, so if you wear ties, make sure they're not wider than the lapels. You'll probably want to button the top two or three buttons.

I'm sixteen and I just purchased a suit. Should I leave those little tags on the sleeve or are they meant to be taken off?

Off! The only people who leave them on deliberately are contes-tants at "voguing" balls who plan to return the clothes and/or want to impress audiences with where the clothes came from and how much they cost. But there's something funny about the idea of leaving them on and having a label that says *mohair* on your wrist. If you do leave the tags on, you may be hailed as the next rebel genius in the fashion business.

I have three days of interviews scheduled for an entry-level position in a high-powered entertainment firm. The woman who interviewed me first suggested I wear a power suit to the following interviews. What's a power suit?

I haven't heard that expression since the 1980s, or at least since Pat Riley left the New York Knicks. *Power suit* refers to a certain look in men's designer clothing. In the eighties the Armani suit, with its strong shoulders, comfortable drape, ventless jacket, and pleated pants was the model of the power suit. I always thought the term might have something to do with the illusion of upper body strength conveyed by the big shoulders, but it probably had more to do with the power-breakfasting, power-lunching, power-cigar-smoking types who wore them. In the late nineties I would venture to guess that a Ralph Lauren or Gucci suit might be just as power packed, but I'm guessing here. My advice is to just look your best. Wear the smartest suit you can. A three-button single-breasted model looks modern. If you have only one suit, make sure to accessorize with different-colored shirts and ties for all three days. Chances are if the suit is a plain color, no one will notice you're wearing the same one each day.

What's a ticket pocket? What's a fob pocket?

A ticket pocket is a small, flapped pocket that's found above the right-side pocket on a man's suit or sport jacket. Originally it was intended for carrying a railroad ticket; today it's intended to show you're wearing a British-style suit. The fob pocket is a handy little

pocket found on the waistband seam of men's trousers. It was originally intended for carrying a pocket watch when one wasn't
wearing a vest. The fob pocket is usually invisible, so it's a good
place to keep folding money when venturing into dicey neighbor-
hoods. It's also called a watch pocket or narcotics pocket.

Okay, what's Savile Row and what's a bespoke suit?

Savile Row is a street in London where most of the town's great
custom tailors are located. An off-the-rack suit is what it sounds
like: it's made for a fit model, then it's altered to fit you. A made-to-
measure suit is one step up, where certain measurements are input
at the factory. A bespoke suit is a suit that's made for you from
scratch. It is totally custom, with dozens of measurements taken
and usually two fittings required. Bespoke suits are expensive, but
when you compare the cost with the price of high-end off-the-rack
suits from major designers, they give good value. When you're
buying a big-name designer suit you're paying a lot for the name,
for marketing and advertising. You're buying a fashion look. When
you buy a custom-made suit you're buying a very labor intensive
garment that is, theoretically, made to your exact measurements
and specifications. Most Savile Row tailors offer amazing expertise
and quality. If you don't get fat, a Savile Row suit will last a lifetime.
And if you do get fat, most of the tailors will fix it for you free of
charge.

Why don't the buttons on the cuff of a man's jacket function?

Sometimes they do. Often Savile Row tailors or other bespoke
clothing makers fashion working buttonholes. They come in handy
if you're doing a charcoal sketch or making a pizza while wearing
your suit and you want to roll up the sleeves. Leaving the first
button unbuttoned is a subtle signal to the other guys that your suit
was made for you. But a tailor will open up your buttonholes for a

fairly modest fee, giving you the Jean Cocteau/Duke Ellington hard-working dandy look.

I like the look of tweed suits. Where can I wear one?

In England, home of the tweed suit, it's strictly a country thing. It's not for wearing to the office. In America you can probably get away with it, particularly if you work at an ad agency or in a less-conservative-type office. It's definitely the perfect look for professorial types. Tweed is handsome but toasty. I'd save it for those cold winter days.

I like the look of a boutonniere, a flower in the lapel. Is this only for weddings?

I guess it's come to this. We live in an age where brow piercing and slave tattoos are normal and wearing a flower in your lapel is weird. So be it. Actually, wearing a flower in one's lapel is a nice, time-honored custom. It seems best for social occasions. Or at least, I wouldn't want to be the first junior executive in the office to try it out, but if you're the boss, bloom on.

I'm in the market for a suit. I'm confused by the whole vent situation. Some have a vent in the middle of the back of the jacket, some have a vent on each side, some don't have any. Why is this? What's best?

If you look at old Hollywood movies, you rarely see a vent. This may be the best look for a jacket, an uninterrupted silhouette. This look was popular through the eighties and into the nineties in fashionable designer clothing such as Armani, Ferre, or Zegna. The single-vented look is very American, and it's a traditional part of the boxy, natural-shoulder Brooks Brothers–style jacket. If you walk behind a crowd on Wall Street today, chances are you're going to see more single vents than anything else. Today a lot of fashionable dudes are going back to the traditional British look, the double vent. This cut traces its heritage back to the equestrian days. If you were riding to the hounds or riding with the Bengal Lancers in India, you were wearing double vents. These are located on the sides, toward the back, and they're perfectly located for mounting a horse (or a Harley). They also work well with the shaped silhouette of British tailoring, and they're practical. If you put your hand in your pants pocket, it doesn't hike up the whole jacket. The vent gives you instant access. It also performs better sitting on things besides horses, like the chair in your office.

Do double-vented suits look good on short guys, or are we limited to single-vented suits?

Double vents are more stylish than single vents, and height shouldn't have much to do with how they look. What could make a difference is the length of your torso versus the length of your legs. If you have a longer torso and shorter legs, a long vent could accentuate it. If the vents look long, a tailor can shorten them easily.

I'm 6′4″ and 225 pounds. I like Prada, Versace, and other designer clothes, but they don't make anything remotely my size. Where can I find something stylish and affordable in larger sizes?

If you live in a big city like New York or L.A., it shouldn't be a huge problem. Stores like Barneys carry fashionable clothes in larger sizes. There are also stores that cater to athletes in many large cities. Rich athletes often go for the fashion-forward stuff, so try to find where your local power forward or tight end picks up his four-button suits or Nehrus. Perhaps your best bet is finding a good custom tailor who can copy the look that you like. It's often no more expensive than buying designer stuff, since tailors don't have huge overheads and advertising budgets. In New York there's a tailor named Mohan who dresses a lot of the Knicks. I'm sure there's an equivalent tailor near every major sports franchise.

Is a navy suit wrong for a funeral?

No. Traditionally black is worn for mourning, but if you don't have a black suit, you can wear dark gray or navy. Sporty suits, like plaids or tweeds, aren't really appropriate. Just look as subdued as you can.

Is it possible for a real old suit to look good? I once wore an old suit of my dad's to a wedding, and everyone asked me if it was from Zegna.

Definitely. I have Dad's Hickey-Freeman from the early sixties that is totally up to the moment—three buttons, slim lapels, plain-front high-waisted trousers. As long as the fabric isn't worn, an old suit can be eminently groovy. Designers are notorious flea-market freaks.

What do you wear with a brown suit?

Many colors of shirts go with a brown suit. Brown is not one of them. Brown on brown is a look that went out with the Nazi Party. White, powder blue, and medium blue are classics. Beige, ivory, or soft pinks and yellows can work well. I'd tend to avoid red, strong yellow, orange, or purple. But when it comes to picking a shirt, your complexion is just as important as the color of your suit. If your skin is the color of Michael Jordan's, you'll look great in an orange shirt. If your skin is the color of Larry Bird's, you might want to stick with powder blue. Wearing green makes some people look green. By the way, brown suits call for brown shoes (or brown and white during summer).

What kind of shirt and tie goes with a dark gray suit, besides the boring white shirt and red tie?

If you wear a white shirt with a red tie, you risk being mistaken for a member of Congress. The good thing about a gray suit is that it goes with just about any color shirt within reason. Pick a color that goes with your complexion and pick a tie that goes with the shirt. Single-breasted suits, especially higher-closing three-button models, give you a little more latitude with sportier-colored shirts. A formal-looking double-breasted suit tends to look better with lighter-colored solids, stripes, and checks.

I'm a college student, and for my first internship I just got a moderately priced suit. A friend suggested taking it to a tailor and having my initials sewn on it. He said it will make it seem more in style. This is my first suit. Is he right? If so, where do they go?

No, your initials are not going to add anything but expense. You could have them sewn inside your jacket, but are you likely to misplace your jacket? Sewing them on the outside would not add anything. I once saw initials embroidered on a jacket pocket, but actually they were Al Capone's initials and it was only a movie (with Rod Steiger). You might get some conversation out of it. "Hey, what are those letters on your jacket? Are you a parking lot attendant? Are you a hotel manager?" If it's a fairly good suit, you could upgrade it somewhat by having a tailor make the buttonholes on the jacket cuffs functional. It's a fashion touch that's often done with Savile Row suits.

I have been told not to have my suits cleaned too often, that it's bad for the fabric, but I work in an office where they pick up the smell of cigarette smoke. What's the proper way to care for a suit?

Dry cleaning should be done only when your suit really needs it. Dry cleaning doesn't destroy fabrics, but it's not too good for the buttons. It can also cause deterioration in suits where glue is used to fuse the outer fabric to the inner canvas structure, i.e., most suits. If you spill food on a suit or other woolens, it's time to clean it. That's where the moths will attack. If you have your suit steam pressed between cleanings, it will help get rid of that cigarette smell. You can also steam suits yourself with a hand steamer. Just hang 'em up and steam the wrinkles out. You can also air them outside on a nice day. Just make sure to bring them in before it rains.

Can you wear a suit jacket as a sport jacket?

Bad trend. I guess Letterman started it. Wearing a suit jacket with khakis. Generally it's not working. If you have a nice navy blue suit, then maybe you can wear the jacket as a blazer, but a gray pinstripe and Dockers don't make it, baby. When you look at your suits, just remember the old Al Green song "Let's Stay Together." Why do you think they call it a suit?

Shirt Guys

"Clothes make the man, man makes machines, machines make the clothes."

—Gregory Fleeman

Think of the social implications of the shirt. A blue-collar occupation. A white-collar operation. "He'd give you the shirt off his back." "He lost his shirt in Vegas." The shirt seems to symbolize both the sum of our worldly goods and our social status. So you'd better be wearing the right one, it had better be yours, it had better not be stuffed. And today, as many businesses and social occasions become more informal, the shirt is often the most prominent part of our attire. So when we roll up our sleeves and get to it, it's going to be a lot more noticeable.

I used to wear really baggy pants, so I'm not used to wearing a shirt tucked in and I feel like I look weird tucked in. Should I tuck or not?

Some shirts are designed to be worn untucked. It was a big look for short-sleeved shirts in the fifties. You can tell if it's an "outie" if the tail is neatly squared off. And sometimes there's a little side vent that's a dead giveaway for "don't tuck." Most Hawaiian shirts fall into this category. But all other shirts should be tucked. I think slobbiness may have gotten more prevalent as fatalists approached the millennium. The hefty among us sometimes eschew tucking in an effort to hide the handles or avoid plumber's butt. But this is the sartorial equivalent of a comb-over, and instead of hiding paunch, it broadcasts it. Tuck it in and if it doesn't look good, maybe it's time to check *Abs of Steel* out of the local video store.

When I take my shirts to the laundry how much starch should I get? Should I get them folded or on hangers?

Starching is a matter of taste. I don't use the stuff, myself. Too much starch makes a shirt look stiff, even paramilitary. If you like that crisp look and feel, ask for lightly starched and see if that does it for you. Excessive starching and razor's-edge pressing leads to fraying at the collar and cuffs. As long as you have closet space, shirts on hangers are a better way to go. You avoid that horizontal crease across your chest and arms. Some laundries charge extra for hangers, up to fifty cents a shirt, but many don't. If you're planning on traveling, you might want to get your shirts folded, however, as they're easier to pack.

I had a debate recently on the issue of tucking in golf shirts, Lacoste-type shirts that have a club logo or a corporate logo instead of an alligator. My opponents said that these shirts should always be tucked in. I admit that they might look neater tucked in on the golf course, but I can't imagine that untucked is completely unacceptable, especially since these shirts are often notched on the sides of the bottom hem, lending a finished look.

Personally, I'm for tucking at all times except when such a shirt is worn over a swimsuit. I often wear one untucked when I'm going to and from the beach, but in other cases I think you'll look a lot better tucked. And going untucked on the golf course is right up there with wearing blue jeans or shorty shorts.

When you're wearing a shirt without a tie, how many buttons should be unbuttoned? Is buttoning all the way up to the collar stupid?

The tieless buttoned-up-to-the-top look was big in the late eighties and early nineties. I think it tends to look a little fashion-victim-like, but it can work, especially if you're wearing a dark shirt with a dark jacket or suit. It's okay to wear the second-from-the-top button open if you like, especially in the summer, but the shirt shouldn't be "ajar." If you leave more buttons than two open, you're a candidate for gold chains.

I have a large neck but a thirty-inch waist. Shirts always look baggy on me. What can I do?

Look for tapered shirts with a narrower body. They're available at many outlet stores. Or, if you can afford it, you can have your shirts made to order at better department stores and specialty stores. They don't cost that much more than fine-quality ready-made shirts, but there will probably be a minimum order of at least three shirts. Shirts are also easy to alter, and any tailor should be able to trim them down for you.

Which is better in which situations: button-down collars or plain?
I wear mostly blazers with khakis or wool trousers.

Button-down collars were invented by polo players who didn't like things flapping in the breeze. They are more casual looking and go best with single-breasted jackets. If your blazer (or suit) is double breasted, go for a plain collar. Plain-collared shirts go with any type of jacket, although a spread collar generally looks a bit more formal and goes best with a dressy look.

I'm a recent college grad who will be interviewing for jobs soon. I like the sharp, classy look of French cuffs, but are they appropriate for the job interview process?

In the big world, if you have a good suit, good shirt, and good tie, it doesn't matter whether you link or button—although links go only with a dressy suit, not with a casual suit, like a tweed suit, or a sport jacket. But wearing cuff links is harder than wearing buttons. There's major margin for error if your choice in cuff links is indiscreet. You can't go wrong with a button, but you can go wrong with a cuff link, and there are many more ugly cuff links in this world than handsome, ingenious ones. You can wear something hideously jeweled, you can wear something involving knights in armor, you can find cuff links that scream pimp, you can wear the cuff links of a secret society you don't belong to. But as long as you're wearing something simple, like plain gold links, or elastic knots, you'll be fine. You might even win a few taste points.

However, and that's a big HOWEVER, in many dyed-in-the-wool, traditional, corporate settings it's an unspoken rule that the young bloods wear shirts that button and the senior dudes and old-boys network are linked. Maybe you interview with buttons, serve your apprenticeship in buttons, and then, when partnership is in the wind, a mentor gives you your links to the executive suite. Think about it.

I have a good build, but when I wear nice shirts I look like a slob because they always come untucked. Am I doing something wrong?

No, you're probably just long waisted. Not all shirts are the same length. I just went through my closet with a tape measure and found a four-inch range of variation in length from collar to tail. You might have your shirt salesperson measure the length of various brands in the same size before you buy. You might find more expensive shirts run a little longer because, duh, fabric costs money. If that doesn't work, maybe you need to find a tall-man's shop. Some people of average height are tall people from the butt up.

Is it considered a faux pas to wear a short-sleeved shirt to the office?

That would seem to depend on your office. If your office is Mission Control at NASA, a white short-sleeved shirt would seem almost required. And I'm sure it's considered quite snazzy among retro-hip Silicon Valley programmers. But at most offices, it's the mark of the dork.

I'm tired of the solid-shirt, solid-tie, Swingers look. What can I do to spruce up my shirt and tie options?

Boldly enter the world of striped and checked shirts. It may be scary at first, but if you relax and pay attention, you'll come out looking good. Your solid ties will look good with patterned shirts. Just make sure the color combos are friendly. If you're color-blind, don't be afraid to ask for help. Your solid shirts will go with all kinds of ties—stripes, plaids, polka dots, prints—as long as your color combos don't start strobing on you. As a rule you don't mix stripes and stripes. But once you're into it, you'll enjoy breaking the rules. Think of the fun you can have with plaid on plaid. And as you become more knowledgeable you can start wearing the ties of clubs and British Regiments you don't belong to, posh schools you didn't attend, the tartans of clans and coats of arms of families you aren't a part of, secret societies where you remain uninitiated. The tie, often considered the sign of bourgeois conformity, is actually the most individualistic and potentially transgressive element of the wardrobe.

Some of my shirts have a loop of the same fabric on the back. What is this?

When I was in high school we called it the fruit loop, and some rude boys have referred to it as a fag tag and sought to destroy this handy appendage, but actually it's called a locker loop. It's so you can hang your shirt from a hook without it getting messed up. Jean Paul Gaultier has featured them for years, even on his suits, and they work.

Is it appropriate to wear a button-down-collar shirt with a tie and jacket for a business meeting? If so, when?

The button-down look used to be considered more casual, but today it often passes for business dress at the highest levels, like say Al Gore. Button-down shirts are more acceptable with single-breasted jackets. They don't make it with double-breasted. I don't wear them with suits. I wear them with sport jackets or a single-breasted blazer, but I'm a conservative, old-style Style Guy.

I was given an official NHL hockey jersey as a gift. What do I wear it with? Is there a special shirt I'm supposed to wear underneath it?

As far as I can tell, NHL jerseys are generally worn to hockey games. They tend to go with acid-washed jeans. And don't forget to paint your face in the team colors. What do you wear under it? There's no correct answer, but there is always the traditional "Kiss Me, I'm Irish" or "Beam Me Up, Scotty" T-shirt.

Guys in Ties

"Bond mistrusted anyone who tied his tie with a Windsor knot. It showed too much vanity. It was often the mark of a cad."

—Ian Fleming, *From Russia with Love*

Ties have a bad name. They're considered corporate, conformist. They're unnecessary but sometimes they're indispensable. A lot of jobs require a suit and tie. People look at this as a chore, but actually ties are the one way that many working men can express their own aesthetic.

I'm wondering if slim ties are back in style and if the monochromatic look—blue shirt, blue tie—is still popular.

According to the moment mavens, we are in a slim-tie moment. This is not a movement I'm about to join, but if you're young and slim and have the right threads to go along with it, yes, you may. The one thing to watch for is the width of your jacket lapels. No matter what the trend, skinny ties don't make it with big lapels. The rule I live by is that the width of the tie should approximate the width of the lapel. Skinny ties look right with that fifties greaser slim lapel, daddy-O.

I was never much of a tie wearer, but I just started a new job where a tie is required. What's the best way to clean and care for them?

Always hang it on a rack when you're not wearing it. Unless you get something on it, a tie doesn't need much care. For grease spots, my favorite tie stain, I try K2r spray-on spot remover. The powder lifts the grease, then you brush it off. If that doesn't work, use the best dry cleaner you can find. If they specialize in ties, there's usually a sign to that effect. There's an excellent service in New York called Tiecrafters, which will save ties that just seem way too gravy laden to live another day. They'll service you by mail, but you have to save up four dirty ties to do business with them (212-629-5800; www.tieclean.com).

Are tie clips uncool?

Not necessarily. Tie clips can be droll, ironic, or a complete Dada fashion statement. Of course, the kind with teeth can chew on your ties, so exercise caution. Style Guy has two tie clips in his collection. One, a fine sterling silver golf club received as a gift, will be worn someday, should he ever score a hole in one. The other, a Huckleberry Hound clip (with teeth) will probably just be held on to as an investment. A word of warning: Some people think that tie clips are a sign of psychosis (see Alfred Hitchcock's *Strangers on a Train*).

Are tie tacks uncool?

Yeah.

Bow tie: Yes please, or no thanks?

With a tuxedo, yes please. There's nothing more ridiculous than going to a black-tie affair with no tie. It's morally wrong. With a suit, hey, go for it. It will certainly set you apart from the pack, unless, of course, you're working with Farrakhan. Actually I think those cats from the Nation of Islam look sharp. Nobody's going to call them dweebs.

If you do wear a bow tie, you probably want to wear it with a button-down-collar shirt. And don't get one of those big butterfly bow ties. You'll look like Rip Taylor. Go for the thinner, more Pee-wee-style straight-edge bow tie. Just don't tie it Pee-wee neat. Bow ties are a bit eccentric, so they should be a bit asymmetrical.

Clip-on bow ties should be worn only if they contain a water-squirting device.

I never know how long to make my necktie when I wear one. Sometimes I see men with ties that are the wrong length, and they look silly.

They say that the tie should cover your belt buckle. I'd say it should at least be in that vicinity. I've bought a few great vintage ties that have come up quite short, and it's true they look off, but they look fine under a vest or a V-necked sweater.

What do you think of the matching-shirt-and-tie look?

It's very theatrical. It's very Hollywood. It's really hard to carry it off. But when it's done well it can look very cool. Maybe twenty guys in America can carry it off, including *Details'* L.A. editor, David Keeps, who does it with polka dots.

Is wearing an ascot pretentious?

An ascot is part of traditional morning dress, so you may find your-self wearing one if you're in the party at a fancy daytime wedding. The casual variety is usually worn loosely around the neck under a shirt. I've always thought they usually accompanied some kind of attitude problem, being worn by guys like Higgins on *Magnum P.I.*

If I encountered one worn with a tweed jacket with leather patches on the elbows by a man smoking a pipe, I might even cross the street. But Fred Astaire and Cary Grant carry them off nicely in the movies, and I've seen some older dudes around Manhattan where the look was definitely working. Last Christmas I was given an ascot from Charvet by my agent. I wore it with a white piqué shirt and black velvet jacket on New Year's Eve and I looked marvelous. Of course, I have gray hair and I was not pretending.

Guys Wearing the Pants

"You should never have your best trousers on when you go out to fight for freedom and truth."

—Henrik Ibsen

Here's where you keep the family jewels. Here's where the barn door is located. Here's where you stow your wallet, your key, your currency. Here is where your manhood makes a subtle (or not so subtle) appearance. Wearing the pants is a manly thing. Wear them with pride and intelligence.

Where does the term chinos come from?

Style Guy once theorized that chinos were invented in Chino, California, a town some thirty miles east of Los Angeles, where a famous state prison is located. According to my encyclopedia, Chino's main industries are textiles and mobile homes. I figured that chinos were probably first made there by local textile mills for the local prison inmates, then caught on with the general populace. I placed a call to the Chino Chamber of Commerce to ask if chinos had indeed originated there, but the gentleman who answered the phone had never heard of chino trousers. (He was familiar with the term khakis, but uncomfortable with the topic of men's trousers in general.) He kindly referred me to the Chino Historical Society, and the lady who answered there was more emphatic—she had never heard of there being a textile industry in Chino, California. There was once a sugar beet factory, but that was a long time ago. This dead end sent me back to the books, and finally in *The American Heritage Dictionary of the English Language* I found a note that said *chino* is American Spanish for *toasted*. Chinos are the color of toast. And so it seems entirely appropriate, when toasting, to substitute *chino chino* for *cin cin*.

What's the story with permanent press? I think it used to be polyester. Now they have cotton permanent press. Is it any good?

It has its advantages. A lot of manufacturers now offer cotton permanent-press khakis and pants. They're made with a process that involves baking the fabric with enzymes. I tested them out, and they do stay pressed. The downside is that they aren't as soft as regular cotton pants and sometimes they act like lint magnets. I wore a navy pair to a restaurant, and the napkin made dandruff all over my lap.

I don't know whether to get cuffs on my trousers or not. Please help me.

This is a taste thing. What looks good to you? The conventional wisdom is that if you want to look taller or to make your legs look longer, wear plain bottoms. I've always liked cuffs (or turnups, as they call them in the U.K.) because I like the look and I often find dimes in the cuffs, but lately I've been wearing plain bottoms when I play golf and I notice the house is a lot less sandy. (Hey, I just read that cuffs were invented by members of the British House of Commons in 1893. Finally, a fashion not invented by the Duke of Windsor! This may influence your decision.) By the way, cuffs are always taboo with tuxedo trou.

I'm a big guy—6'1", 195 pounds. My legs aren't fat, but they're too big. How can I de-emphasize them and not look like I'm wearing a tent?

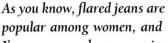

Actually, slimmer trousers might help. Not skinny-leg pants, but plain-front (pleatless) pants that aren't baggy. A higher-rise waist can help, too, making your legs look longer. Dark colors are slimming. So are vertical stripes or narrow-wale corduroys.

As you know, flared jeans are popular among women, and I've seen several guys wearing them. Is this a new trend?

One of the hottest pants looks in recent years happened when young girls discovered men's low-rise flared slacks from the early seventies (obviously in small sizes). These look especially nice on a nice bod with a little belly showing and inspired a whole design revival. I've always thought that flared jeans looked okay on guys, even when they were out, if they fit your body and you're wearing the appropriate footwear, boots. I confess to owning several pairs of vintage Lily Pulitzer flowered golf pants, and although there are many areas in America where I would be beaten up on sight for wearing them, I do dig that slight flare. It seems to me the one early-seventies men's fashion development with some enduring cool.

I like the way guys' pants look in old movies. What's the difference?

Until the fifties, men's pants usually had a higher rise; that is, the waist actually went up somewhere near the waist. They showed less shirt and were usually looser fitting and held up by braces (suspenders). It can be a very flattering look, especially if you're long in the torso. Also, you fuller-figured guys will find that higher-waisted pants will prevent your gut from spilling out over your pants in the front or giving you plumber's butt in the back. Some designers have been doing a higher rise. I got some great khakis from Calvin Klein Collection a few seasons back, and I think the Ralph Lauren Purple Label offers a higher waist. You can usually order a higher-rise trouser if you get your suits made to measure, which you can often do with fine suits at no extra charge during certain times of the year at better department stores like Bergdorf Goodman, Barneys, Saks, or Neiman Marcus. You can also have a tailor do some for you, and it will cost you less than a prefab pair from one of those hot Italian designers. I like the look of the old pants that were made to be held up by braces, with the waistband raised in the back where the braces attach.

Being 5′6″, I have a hard time finding a proper-fitting inseam. The shortest inseam in most stores is 30. Hemming jeans never produces the same look as the original cuff. How do I solve this problem?

Roll the mothers up. They are blue jeans, they go many places, but they are not formal trousers, young bud. If you're a stickler for no roll, however, a good tailor, maybe even at your dry cleaner, can do a double row of stitching at the bottom that looks like the real thing—the only trick is matching the thread.

I think acid-washed jeans are the ugliest invention of the twentieth century. What were they thinking?

When I was a lad, acid was something one dropped. In one's self, not in a washing machine. In that pristine era blue jeans acquired their tonality from washing in nothing stronger than a heavy dose of Tide. Of course, there were those kids who just couldn't wait for time to age their jeans to the proper patina, and so they used bleach to speed the process. This never really looked right. Then, probably by accident, somebody used too much bleach and came up with a sort of tie-dyed, unevenly bleached effect. This caught on with girls for a while, but jeans remained naturalistic until the advent of stonewashed jeans in the eighties. This process, invented by an Italian denim mill, used pumice stones to simulate natural wear, and they came fairly close. Next came the infamous acid wash. This was a real departure because no longer was the goal a natural faded look. The object would seem to be to create jeans that look like they were left out in acid rain and then hung out to dry on a line underneath a hole in the ozone layer.

In fact acid-washed jeans aren't acid-washed at all. They are washed in an alkaline substance, the chemical opposite of acid. Manufacturers seem to have decided that acid-washed sounded better, alkaline jeans sounding too much like batteries. If jeans washed in actual acid came into contact with the in-fact alkaline-washed acid-washed jeans, a dangerous explosion might result, particularly if it were raining out. What will replace the toxic look? Today Italian mills are working on hand-sanded jeans. These will be worn down where jeans wear naturally, the knees, the fly, the butt.

Now that I've gotten into slim flat-front pants, where do I put my loose change, wallet, and keys?

How about a male purse from Louis Bijan, a fluorescent fanny pack, or a good old-fashioned money belt? Not really you? Sport jackets have lots of pockets. And if your wallet is too fat to sit on, maybe you shouldn't carry your money in it, or more than one picture of your dog. How many credit cards do you really need at once? And how many keys? Try editing your stuff and giving your loose change to those who need it more than you do. Several good leather companies make card cases that will hold a few credit cards, your driver's license and registration, and what you really need. These slim carriers will fit in your shirt pocket, inside jacket pocket, or side pocket without bulging or making you sit funny.

I like the way my jeans look and feel after they've been washed, but after one wear they're baggy in the knees. Can I revive them without washing clean jeans?

You could spritz them with a little water and throw them in the dryer for a few minutes, if you have a dryer handy. That should tighten them up nicely. If not, hang them in the bathroom and run the shower on full hot for a few minutes so the room steams up. (This is also an effective way of taking the creases out of a suit.)

After one wearing, my sharkskin trousers get wicked creases across the front. Solutions?

You could get a trouser press for your home, but they're big and not cheap. Or you could get a small steamer, a cheap, handy, portable appliance that all fashionable girls own. Hang up your pants or suit, give it a quick steam, and you look as fresh as Crockett and Tubbs. But be warned, if you're creasing across the crotch, that's a pretty good indication you may be wearing pants a wee bit too tight.

I wear boots, and whenever I wear loose jeans they're too tight at the bottom, and when I try baggy jeans they seem exaggeratedly large. What are the right jeans for me?

You're looking for a boot cut. Lots of makers offer them. Why not try the jeans real cowboys wear—Lee Riders and Wrangler.

When I get my pants tailored they always give me the leftover fabric. What am I supposed to do with it?

Save it in case you fall off your skateboard in your suit or drop a spliff in your lap. Then you can give the cloth to a good weaver, and the trousers or jacket may survive without visible scars. These leftovers are also great for accessories shopping. You can carry a swatch around to shop for shirts and ties without schlepping a whole suit.

Um, how old is too old to wear a hip-hop look?

I've been trying to find out what the maximum age is for being initiated into the Crips and the Bloods, but nobody will tell me.

Lately I've noticed a lot of men not wearing belts. Not just with jeans, but with shorts and khakis. Isn't the rule to wear a belt?

I always think that if there are loops, you should use them, unless you're sporting suspenders. It's not a rule, but belts are cool. They don't have to actually hold your pants up.

I haven't worn jeans in the past three years because I think they are uncomfortable, but I'd like to go for a less preppie look. How can I dress down and still be presentable?

Chinos don't have to look preppie. Picasso wore khakis, right? You can hip up your preppie look with a little canny accessorizing. Go for a beret, spectator shoes, something that used to be an alligator. Add something nonmainstream from agnès b., Paul Smith, A.P.C., or maybe Comme des Garçons to your Gap/Brooks Brothers uniform and you'll turn from a preppie to a virtual Pepé Le Pew. Something vintage and excellent will tone down your bourgeois glare. By the way, if it's comfort below the waist you're after, stick with pleats and don't mount the flat-front bandwagon.

I'm a golfer and I like the old knickers look. Am I insane?

Not necessarily. The late, great Payne Stewart, the only golfer on the pro tour to wear knickers, sometimes looked a bit insane, but was sane enough to get the National Football League to pay him a fortune to wear knickers and an old-style cap in the colors of the team closest to where the tournament was played. The result was that Stewart often looked more colorful than a traditional linksman. Of course, traditional knickers are available, but if you want to wear them, I suggest you look something like Sean Connery. And if you're going to wear the knickers, you should probably go all the way and wear a tweed cap, a loose-fitting long-sleeved shirt, and a tie. Good luck to you.

I always have a lot of change rattling around in my pants pockets. I think it even contributes to wearing holes in them. What can I do? I hate those little change purses.

I hate change. I always use my credit card at pay phones. (Just make sure there are no peepers stealing your number—a common criminal activity at train stations, bus terminals, and airports.) I try to avoid getting stuck with copper and faux silver by giving bigger tips to taxi drivers, giving to beggars on the street. What's left when I get home I save in huge jars that accumulate for years, except for the quarters, which go to my cleaning woman for the laundromat. In other words, I have no idea. I just wish they'd stop making pennies.

If you're not wearing Dockers, are you just wearing pants?

No, you may in fact be wearing trousers.

What is the advantage of a button fly?

Safety.

Guys in Underwear (or Not)

"Semper ubi, sub ubi."

—proverbial

Nothing comes between me and my Calvins. Or my Charvet French-cut boxers, or my black Paul Smith briefs with the button fly, or my full-cut Brooks Brothers tartan boxers. Men aren't about lingerie, but underwear still makes a statement. It says more about your underlying aesthetic than anything that readily meets the naked eye.

I'm a nineteen-year-old university student. My roommate makes fun of me because I always wear white briefs. He says only men over forty and geeks wear briefs. I've tried boxers, but I don't feel comfortable in them. He also says girls prefer boxers. I've always thought of underwear as a mere necessity. What's the truth?

The truth is women prefer men who don't criticize other men's underwear. If your white briefs make you feel clean and secure, wear them proudly. There are many men who express themselves through colorful and stylish underwear, perhaps compensating for a drab exterior. There are many men who wear wilder skivvies to surprise and delight their most intimate associates. And there are men such as yourself whose concerns lie elsewhere. Fortunately, there's room for all of us in this great land of underwear opportunity.

I'm a girl and I disagree with you on "tight whities." I don't like white briefs and neither do my friends. Boxers are much sexier.

I, too, generally prefer boxers, especially if someone might see them. But some young guys like the security afforded by briefs. For instance, in case of a spontaneous boner, they are much more helpful in keeping Mr. Johnson in place. Aesthetically, of course, you are quite right, miss. I myself have a magnificent collection of French-cut boxers from Charvet and fuller American-cut boxers from ye olde Brooks Brothers. I've got colors, stripes, tartans. And I also have some very seductive longer briefs with buttons from Paul Smith. I was just defending a poor guy's right to personal choice when criticized by a college roommate who should mind his own underwear.

My wife often points out that I'm dressed to the left or right. My old girlfriends also noted my blatant package. I'm big but not enormous. I prefer boxers. I'm not parading around semierect, but I'm embarrassed. What's the answer?

Briefs, or at least snugger-fitting shorts. Bigger pants with more pleats. Jeans or plain-front narrow trousers aren't for you, big boy. Some pants have a longer rise than others, i.e., a greater length from waist to crotch. Try to wear a longer rise and don't let them ride up. And make sure your fly is up. Only your wife will know the awful truth.

This is a women's question, but it has been on my mind. My girl-friend says her workplace is too conservative for her to wear thongs underneath suits. I don't see VPL, visible panty line, as a conservative versus liberal issue.

I can see why you are troubled by this. Unless her job requires regular strip searches or she works in an oval-like office, I can't imagine how anyone would know she was wearing a thong. The whole point of a thong, aside from the titillation factor it provides when the pants are removed, is that it makes underwear invisible under clothing. There could be more to this panty-line issue than meets the eye.

I don't wear underwear. I find it liberating and more comfortable. I began seeing a girl who thinks it's disgusting and disrespectful. Am I wrong to "go commando"?

It's a free country, but I vote for underwear. For one thing there's that old grade school bathroom chant, "No matter how much you shake and dance, the last few drops end up in your pants." Better your underpants than your overpants. I also question the comfort of "commandoism." Since most of us have been nonconsensually deprived of our foreskins, don't those soft, cushioning under-drawers help us retain sensitivity where it matters most? Besides, underwear can be very handsome, and if it gives your woman pleasure to unwrap that extra layer, why not give in?

I'm eighteen and last summer I switched to wearing boxer shorts like my friends. Most of them stick their shirts inside their boxers and let them stick outside their pants. They even buy bigger boxers so they'll show more. My parents say it's underwear and shouldn't show. Is showing underwear fashionable or stupid?

I remember a few years ago when *stupid* was a synonym for *fashionable*. This was also the period when low-rider pants, high-rider boxers were popular. In those days it was a hip-hop attitude inspired by the jailhouse no-belt policy. Today emerging underwear is sported by white suburbanites with attitude. Stupid seems a lot less fashionable these days.

I've recently discovered the comfort of ribbed tank-top underwear, the kind Harvey Keitel wears in **City of Industry**. *My friends think these are the mark of trailer-park white trash. What do you think?*

What we used to call "Italian T-shirts" certainly have their charm. I wouldn't recommend them for male breast-reduction candidates, but if you've got the body for them, they can be sexy undershirts or a casual tropical outerwear choice. If your friends really hate them, you could screen some old Brando films for them and practice lines like "I coulda been a contenda" and "Stella!" But for a second opinion, see below.

I'm a girl who's about to break up with her boyfriend because he thinks it's cool to walk around in public in those nasty undershirt-like tank tops. If it's too late for me, maybe you can save other women the embarrassment of going through a summer like this.

Men, why do you think this sort of garb is called by some a "wifebeater"? I mean, sure it looked good on Marlon Brando in *On the Waterfront*, but are you Marlon Brando and are you on the waterfront? Chances are, even young Marlon didn't wear these on the street. There's a reason that undershirts are called undershirts, guys. I assume you're not talking about designer tanks of the sort sold by Gucci, Dolce & Gabbana, or Diesel, which have something going on fashionwise. These can look okay in less formal public situations, but not if the guy's body is late-model Brando.

I wear button-downs, and my T-shirt shows underneath. Is this okay? Should I not wear an undershirt with these shirts?

This is the reason V-necked T-shirts were invented. If you like to wear a T-shirt but don't like them to show, buy V necks. They weren't manufactured for years, but now they're back in fashion mainstream. (The guys on *Friends* wear them.) Maybe you should stock up in case the fickle winds of fashion blow them away again.

I live in the midwest and freeze my butt every winter. I've worn thermal long johns to work, and that keeps me comfortable en route, but the office is overheated, so I either have to take off my underwear in the men's room or swelter all day. What's the answer?

Silk long underwear keeps you warm in an arctic blast, but it's comfortable at room temperature, too. It's also thin enough that it doesn't affect the fit of your clothes. It feels great against your skin, so it makes good lounging-around wear, too. Silkies can be had at outdoor stores like Eddie Bauer or through catalogs like L. L. Bean.

*What's your opinion of rolled-up T-shirt sleeves? My friends say it
makes you look like an idiot and a poseur. I like the look.*

Idiot? I'd say it makes you look like you're going to a costume party
as the Fonz or a member of Sha Na Na. The only reasonable excuse
for rolling up a T-shirt sleeve is if it's to hold a pack of Camel regulars or Lucky Strikes. (Or, in Europe, Gauloises regulars.) And even
then, you may roll up only one.

Formal Guys

"Lenin in a top hat and frock coat would be a far greater anomaly than a Grand Master of Tibet or a Zulu chief in that costume."

—Wyndham Lewis

Formality isn't what it used to be. Today most people are utterly confused by the concepts of "formal," "semiformal," "evening dress," or "black-tie," not to mention such things as "white-tie," "morning dress," etc. These days invitations are more likely to say "festive," or "shirts and shoes required," or something that would have been unimaginable fifty years ago.

I think a little more formality would be a good thing. It's a good discipline. And I know that many of my dear readers will think I'm full of it on this count, but I really think that extravagantly nonconformist dress is often the most conformist. In black-tie, as in life, it's the subtleties that truly set you apart.

Tuxedos, buy or rent?

Renting a tux and the fixings will probably set you back between $75 and $100. A decent new tux and accessories will probably cost a minimum of $700. Figure out your life for the next few years and you do the math. You might also keep in mind that good low-mileage formal wear can often be found in thrift shops at a fraction of the cost of a new suit. Some will look retro. But since every style tux has come and gone and come again, there's one out there that will look au courant. I guess at the moment that would be early sixties. The advantages of owning are obvious. You'll be sure to have something that fits, and you'll save schlepping time. I'm a believer in tux ownership. Bob Hope's business card read "Have tux, will travel." I think just seeing it there in the closet can inspire opera going or Academy Award winning.

What kind of shirt should I wear with a tux?

A tuxedo shirt with a turned-down collar and pleats or a piqué front looks great. You wear studs, not buttons, although there are some nice modern tux shirts that don't have any visible closure in the front and they are A-OK. Ruffles are okay if you're going for a Vegas retro statement, and you can carry it off. I'm leaving that job for others. Personally, and it's okay to get personal in matters of taste, I hate the look of wing collars with black-tie. It's a white-tie shirt in a black-tie world. If you look like Clifton Webb or William Powell, you might be able to get away with it, but generally a wing collar looks like you're trying too hard. And anything else looks like you've been nominated for Best Special Effects in a Foreign Language Movie.

What kind of tie goes with a tux?

One that matches the fabric of the lapels. It shouldn't be pretied unless you're wearing pretied shoes. And it shouldn't be huge. Big butterflies remind me of caterpillars. An inch-width tie is hard to find, but you have your whole life ahead of you.

I'm a professional musician. I play a lot of weddings, and I prefer to wear white-tie and tails to a tuxedo. Someone recently told me this was inappropriate for day wear. True?

White-tie is full evening dress—a swallow-tailed coat and matching trousers with a formal white shirt, white vest, and white tie. A tux works for both day and night. Formal day weddings often call for morning dress, which combines a swallow-tailed coat with striped trousers. Codes aren't what they used to be, but if it's an all-occasions look you want, go with the tuxedo.

The little tab in the middle of the torso of a tuxedo shirt: what does it fasten to? Also there's a vent a couple of inches long, not a pocket, over the left breast. What's that for?

Sounds like you have an English-style tux shirt. American manufacturers have pretty much dispensed with these nice little details. The tab loops over the button on the inside front of your trousers to keep the shirt from riding up when you do the frug, the monkey, the alligator, the pogo, or the muskrat ramble. This vent you speak of is probably a hankie pocket that is still stitched closed. Open it up and you'll be able to carry a hankie in your shirt and, on Oscar night, a couple of Xanaxes.

What kind of shoes do you recommend with a tuxedo?

If you're a crooner by trade, if you have a James Bond fixation, if you wear black-tie frequently, or if you just have money to burn, you'll wear evening shoes. These are always black; they may be slip-ons or plain tie shoes. Sometimes there's patent leather involved. They should always be polished. Evening slip-ons sometimes come with bows. If you're sporting bows, they should match the stripe on your trousers, i.e., grosgrain or satin. You may also wear plain-toed black dress shoes, or even slender cap toes. Wing tips or bulky oxfords look too big and clunky. Penny loafers look too casual. Classic Brooks Brothers–style tassel loafers are okay. Slipper-type shoes in black calf or velvet are often worn by experienced lounge lizards. I like 'em cause they're comfy. Sometimes they have an embroidered emblem on the vamp. Belgian Shoes in New York offers initials, crowns, or the masks of tragedy and comedy. New York's New Republic had some natty-looking death's-head slippers in velvet for that elegantly creepy Transylvanian touch, but the store has given up the ghost.

I just got an invitation that says "creative black-tie." What does that mean?

It means dressing like the fashion victims you see on the Oscars. Tuxedos with black shirts. Tuxedos with no ties. Tuxedos with bolo ties. Personally I believe the whole point of black-tie is for the men to be in uniform and let the ladies provide the variety. Creativity in black-tie is best expressed in the studs and cuff links in one's shirt and one's choice of shoes. Style Guy believes that wearing formal dress without a tie is like playing classical music with a kazoo. In the late sixties and early seventies a lot of people thought a turtleneck and beads was an acceptable substitute for a dress shirt and tie. Twenty years later, Sonny Bono was a member of Congress.

Some tuxes have shiny satin lapels, others have a flatter-looking fabric. What's the diff?

Grosgrain is the other fabric. It looks like ribbon. Either look is correct, although a shawl-collar tux should have only a satin lapel. Tux trou have a strip of fabric that matches the lapels of the jacket down the outer seam of the leg. If your lapels and pants feature grosgrain, you should wear a grosgrain cummerbund and tie. If they're satin, wear a satin cummerbund and tie. And one of the nice things about wearing a double-breasted tux is that no cummerbund is necessary.

I'm getting married this September at 4:00 P.M. Are there any rules on time of year or day that a white dinner jacket is acceptable?

White is right from Memorial Day to Labor Day in the north. In the tropics, white is right all year round.

While rummaging through a thrift shop recently, I came up with a vintage navy blue tuxedo. What's up with that?

It's not navy blue, it's midnight blue, a very dark blue that's almost black. The point is that in artificial light it looks blacker than black, or at least more flattering. Very sharp.

I'm getting married in June in Hawaii. What's a snazzy alternative to the monkey suit?

Tuxes are for evening weddings. Morning suits—cutaways coats and striped trousers—are traditional and snazzy for morning weddings. What about cutaway coats and grass skirts?

Foot Guys

"A head waiter once told me: 'I can always tell people by their shoes. People who are only trying to show off and impress you, wear fabulous clothes but are not prepared to spend a lot on their shoes.'"

—The Duke of Bedford's *Book of Snobs*

"Guilty feet, as George Michael tells us, have got no rhythm."

—Stephen Fry

It's almost a cliché that you can tell more about a person by their shoes than any other item of clothing. Feet are the basis, the standard. They take us where we want to go. All our nerves end up there. Support your feet with fine footwear and special care; they support you.

I have bad feet, and I'm comfortable only in sneakers or running shoes. I work in a fairly conservative atmosphere, and I have to spend a lot of time on my feet. I've tried just about every dress shoe. What can I do?

The best course is to see an orthopedic-shoe maker and see what they say they can do for you. Short of that, Nike makes an air-cushioned dress shoe that you might try. There are also many solid-black athletic shoes, like the ones worn by basketball refs that are pretty subtle. You might also try Mephisto shoes. They're made in France, they're pricey, you can't find them everywhere, and unfortunately they have a name tag on the outside of them, but they aren't sneakers, and many bad-feet guys swear they are the world's most comfortable shoes and won't wear anything else. Mephisto also makes a great though far-from-handsome golf shoe.

I'm a height-challenged guy. I'm good looking, well dressed, and, I think, charming, but I can't help but feel I would do better with the ladies if they weren't looking down on me. Are shoes with lifts unthinkable?

Nah. Go for it. I stopped growing just short of six feet, but I test-drove a pair of elevators and loved them. I ordered some Timberland look-alikes from the original "elevator shoe" maker, the Richlee Shoe Company (P. O. Box 3566, Frederick, MD, 800-343-3810). I loved being almost 6′3″ at parties, and nobody seemed to notice. They may have sensed that something was different, but nobody pinned the boots. One day I wore them to an office I frequent, and nobody said a thing. Finally I said, "Notice anything different?" They checked my hair, my clothes, but nobody pegged the elevators. Finally I spilled the beans. "Tall works on you," said one of the ladies. I think maybe women don't notice because they are used to height variations from wearing flats, then wearing heels. Maybe they didn't notice, but maybe there was a subliminal effect. I'm all for 'em, no matter what height you are.

The only problem is that they're not easy to walk in. It's like walking down a hill that never ends. Richlee sells all styles, including golf shoes! You might have to get longer shafts if you wore those. But I did enjoy the boost, and you probably would, too.

I have noticed that in old **Late Night with David Letterman** *episodes, Dave sometimes wears running shoes with suits. Lately he is more traditionally shod. What happened?*

Maybe he grew up? Maybe he stopped running and decided to slow down and smell the roses. Or maybe he realized that while this look might work on a guy in his twenties, it's not so swift on a guy in his forties. Or maybe Mr. Letterman discovered handmade shoes. When you make that much money what else are you going to spend it on? You can own only so many sports cars, and bespoke shoes, at a thousand plus, might be considered a bargain by a man of means with sore feet.

With what kind of pants should cowboy boots be worn?

Cowboy boots should be worn with boot-leg jeans and a horse.

I've always believed that men's accessories—e.g., wallet, belt, and shoes—should be the same shade of leather, either all black or all brown. Am I right?

I'm with you on this, although I draw the line at the wallet, because it comes out only once in a while. I'm currently carrying a black one; however, I think like you, and I have a brown wallet and if I weren't either too lazy or busy, I'd switch all my cards and stuff to it when I'm into a brown-leather mode. I do have black and brown leather gloves for winter to accommodate both shoe choices. I also worry about brown-briefcasing it with my black shoes, and so I'm hoping for Christmas Santa will bring me a black briefcase so I can always be leather coordinated. We're not all rich, but we do the best we can.

What's the best way to suggest to my boyfriend that he shouldn't wear white athletic socks with his loafers on a date?

My mail seems to indicate that this is a common problem, young lady. Ask him if he has a foot disease or infection, since that's the only reason you can imagine he would wear socks that have no dye in them. This may embarrass him into submission. Or you could tell him that you love his Michael Jackson look. Still,

I'm a liberal on white socks. I think they can look okay for a casual daytime look, but never at night on a date unless it's a date to go jogging.

I have five pairs of old shoes that I don't know what to do with. They're not exactly in terrible shape, just worn and rough around the edges. Can I send them somewhere and get money? How could I benefit from giving them to a charity such as the Salvation Army?

Charity is its own reward, son, but if you haven't felt it yet, maybe you should see a shoemaker. A good shoemaker can work wonders, resoling, reheeling, and reconditioning. Good shoes are made to last a long time. Maybe you should have them all redone and then give a little money on their behalf to a worthwhile charity.

I like the look of Guccis, but I have very wide feet. What are my options, besides Nike and New Balance?

Actually Gucci's classic loafer comes in widths up to EEE. Alden, Bally, Bass Weejuns, Bostonians, Church's English Shoes, Clark, Mephisto, Rockport, and Wright, among others, offer narrow and wide sizes. The Wright Shoe Shop of New York stocks many sizes from AAA to EEE (telephone 212-687-3023). Church's English Shoes accepts phone orders (800-221-4540). Two big-shoe stores: Harry's Shoes (800-626-5270) and Lynn Boot & Shoe (800-819-LYNN). If you can afford it, there's the wonderful world of bespoke (i.e., custom-made) shoes. They give the best fit, they are expensive, but they cost less than cars, and if you're mainly a pedestrian, what the hey. Once an individual last is made for your foot, the price goes down for subsequent orders, according to Uncle Scrooge McDuck.

Dress shoes always make my ankles uncomfortable and leave blisters. Aside from getting custom-made shoes (or wearing Doc Martens), how can I make my feet comfortable?

Sounds like you have low-rider ankles. Ask your local shoe repairman to put some pads in the heels of your shoes. They should jack up your ankles enough that they don't chafe.

I recently bought a gray suit and black wing-tip shoes. Are wing tips in or out?

With traditional suits they work. Wing-tip brogues look especially at home with tweed or corduroys. With more high fashion gear like Prada, Gucci, or Dolce & Gabbana they'll probably stick out like a sore foot. Same with jeans. And you definitely don't wear them with formal wear.

I own black Doc Martens. When I wear jeans do I wear white or black socks? Neither feels right.

Maybe your subconscious is screaming out for color. What about red, green, blue, violet, pink, and all of those other colors that can easily intermediate between black leather and blue denim?

It has always been my belief that black and navy blue combinations are a no-no, yet I see many gentlemen in blue suits and black shoes. Am I mistaken, or has the world gone straight to hell?

You're mistaken. Black shoes and belts are a much better choice with navy than brown is. Ask any cop or naval officer. The best evidence of the world having gone to hell is people wearing logo-emblazoned jogging suits on airplanes and in restaurants.

I refuse to wear leather. Could you tell me if there are any stylish shoemakers that make shoes of synthetic leather or other man-made materials?

They may not be too stylish, but the big discount chains like Payless and Kmart sell very inexpensive imitation-leather shoes. For something a bit more fashionable (and probably more comfortable, too) you might try Doc Martens Vege Docs, which come in boot-cut and low-cut models. They are widely available in the U.K. and are also available from some Doc Martens vendors in the U.S. Juliano's offers a similar nonviolent shoe.

Is there really something seriously wrong with khakis, black shoes, and white socks?

No. I might go for brown shoes and colorful socks myself, but black shoes and white socks are within your rights.

I couldn't pass up a recent deal on some expensive black-and-white monk-strap oxfords. I know they'll look good with something, but I don't know what. What?

They'll look splendid with most summer suits or with a blazer and khakis. Just don't let me catch you sports wearing these before Memorial Day. (Unless you're in the tropics, where it's always after Memorial Day.)

What is your opinion of the Adidas-heavy look the lead singer from Korn sports? I am thinking of adopting something like it, but I doubt I'll go that far.

In general, members of the work force rarely go as far as their musical idols, and rightly so, because there's no business like show business. I confess, I have no idea what the lead singer from Korn looks like. I'm sure he's gnarly and everyone is entitled to a phase to transit, but it seems more stylish to improvise your own.

What color shoes (or sneakers) go best when wearing white jeans? I have no clue.

I think white shoes looks best with white trousers. If you wear black shoes, you might look a little bit like a hospital orderly or ice cream salesman. But if you're wearing white jeans, then really casual shoes, say penny loafers, brown or black, look okay. Canvas shoes come in blue, red, and a variety of colors. (I've got camouflage Converse All Stars.) You could match the shoes with your shirt.

I wear loafers with a suit. A friend says they look bad. What do you think?

Maybe they're bad loafers. It used to be that loafers didn't really go with business suits. But we're living in casual times, and loafers can be acceptable. But there are few clothing trends this writer finds more horrifying than the low-vamp, Italianate (Bruno Magli? Banfi?), sock-revealing loafers worn by many businessmen, particularly wealthy businessmen wearing expensive suits and otherwise acceptable gear. They make a guy look like he's auditioning for *Goodfellas II.* Some loafers, such as the traditional Brooks Brothers–style tassel loafer or the high-vamp Alden penny loafer or the high-vamp square-toed Gucci, look just fine with a suit, particularly a single-breasted suit. But life in the business world is hard enough without having to look at men's socks, goddammit.

When I'm trying on shoes and they feel tight, the salesman often says they'll stretch out. Is this true, or should I buy a half size larger?

Slip-on shoes will often stretch out a little bit. Leather will soften up. But shoes should fit pretty well from the beginning. Try several sizes anyway, because in shoes, as in most other categories, sizes differ from manufacturer to manufacturer.

I just bought a pair of ankle-high boots, and after wearing them for a couple of weeks they still make a loud, annoying crunching sound. What could I use to soften the leather?

Neat's-foot oil. The stuff baseball players use on their gloves. It's extracted from the feet of oxen. But don't tell the guy who won't wear leather shoes.

Can I wear the same shoes with both black dress slacks and black jeans?

I think that more formal black shoes, like wing tips or cap toes, don't make it with jeans. Loafers in various styles, except the dreaded low vamp, look good with jeans and slacks.

When the ground is wet and I'm walking, I get splash marks on the back of my pants. What can I do, short of learning to walk all over again?

Timberland-style boots will protect you up to about eight inches above sea level. A pair of rubber Wellington boots will protect you right up to the knee. Of course, you'll be walking around with your pants rolled up, but they'll be clean.

My father, like many men his age, insists on wearing midcalf-length socks with shorts. How can I gently persuade him of the heinousness of this?

Have you tried Polaroiding him? Polaroid him with midcalf socks, then with normal socks. The whole point of midcalf socks is to not show leg when you're wearing a suit. The only other socks that are appropriate with shorts are knee socks. These are worn with shorts on the island of Bermuda, often with a jacket and even a tie. It's a great look. For Bermuda.

I find more and more guys are wearing flip-flops in public. Is this fashionable and/or acceptable?

It seems to be increasingly fashionable. How acceptable is more complicated. I don't think they'll get past many maître d's. For a trip to the beach or a burger joint they would seem acceptable, as long as your feet can bear scrutiny. Toe nails clean and trimmed. No visible fungal farms. Feet clean. But I don't think they make it as evening wear. Flip-flops don't work with a tux, even if they're black.

I think I speak for a lot of women when I beg you to let guys know that they should never wear jean shorts or socks and sandals. It causes loss of interest in many cases. Trust me.

You didn't have to beg. Okay, she's right, guys. It's not a pretty sight.

Why do Gucci loafers have metal horse bits across the front?

So that if you accidentally put your foot in your mouth, you'll be able to stop.

Guys in Hats

"….the hat is the most versatile of man's inventions in clothing, for not only does it indicate the superior or inferior rank or social position of the wearer, but it can also differentiate between the sexes, add sexual attraction to the wearer, indicate the season of the year, and keep the head warm or protect it from the sun or physical injuries. It can also denote the profession and often the age of the wearer as well as his religion or nationality … the hat also often indicates the mood of the wearer."

—Lawrence Langner, *The Importance of Wearing Clothes*

H ats are a sort of religious experience. Nothing marks a Jew more than his yarmulke. Nothing marks a king more than his crown. Nothing marks Dizzy Gillespie more than his beret or Thelonious Monk more than his porkpie hat. Nothing marks the Shriner more than his fez or the Sikh more than his turban. And anyplace I hang my hat is home.

Why don't men wear hats anymore?

I think hats are on a comeback. Hat wearing as a custom was basically stopped by the enormous style impact of John F. Kennedy, who rarely wore a hat. Maybe it was because we were on the verge of the swinging sixties and hair was sprouting and guys didn't want to look like their hatted dads. Kennedy probably eschewed hats because he had a big head and big hair. If he'd been wearing a bulletproof hat in Dallas, he'd be an old lech today.

Today hats are slowly creeping back into general wear. The fact is that some guys look great in them and some don't. I believe that one should wear a baseball cap only when playing baseball. Nothing looks worse than wearing one with a suit and overcoat.

Hats are one stylistic element that separates the men from the boys. Boys can't get away with a real man's hat like a fedora. You've got to have a manly face to swing it. Sinatra was the last great hat man, and millions of men followed his style, brim down in the front, up in the back, tilted down from right to left. In *The Way You Wear Your Hat*, the Sinatra style bio by Bill Zehme, Frank is asked, "How do you know when a hat looks right on you?" Said the Chairman, "When no one laughs."

What kind of hat can a modern guy sport without visible risibility? I've got a bunch of fedoras in my collection: light brown, medium brown, light gray, charcoal. They look great with suits, they keep your head warm, and they set you apart from the hatless millions. The fedora is made of felt. It has a medium brim and a high crown with a crease from front to back. Some particularly fine fedoras have a little elastic cord with a button on it running around the ribbon hatband. On windy days you can plug the button into the buttonhole on your lapel and if the hat goes flying, it won't go far. Unlike Frank I wear the brim up in front and down in the back—either I am trying to look like the great English author and artist Wyndham Lewis (1884–1957) or the Dead End Kids, or I think it looks less serious and more bohemian than the Sinatra style.

American guys should probably avoid British styles like the bowler or the derby, or senior citizen styles like the homburg. The Irish tweed fisherman's hats with a short, usually downturned brim look good with fairly casual clothes. Many young people today are sporting cowboy hats. Sassy women are wearing them with their Prada high heels. I still think you should earn such a hat out there yonder on the range, but they can be cute. The hairy Tyrolean, which features something that looks like a shaving brush emerging from the band, looks a little too, uh, Tyrolean for contemporary wear. Unless, of course, you look like Max von Sydow and like you might be a professional assassin. The old porkpie hat, with a crease around the top of the crown, in straw or felt, was one of Frank's faves, and it is still a winner if you've got the face for it.

My boyfriend thinks that baseball caps are fashion. He even wears them to work with an overcoat in the winter. What is it with guys and baseball caps?

Men like headgear, but are often insecure about wearing a real man's hat. Maybe they are afraid of giving up the trappings of youth. I think caps are generally for boys, or men at sport. Hats are for men on their way to work or going out on the town. Maybe you can take your guy hat shopping and give him some help picking out something that looks good. For casual wear there's always the old Ben Hogan–style golf cap. Maybe leave pictures of Gary Cooper or Cary Grant in fedoras lying around his apartment. Learn the lyrics to George and Ira Gershwin's "They Can't Take That Away from Me" and sing it in his ear: "The way you wear your hat . . ."

I kind of like the look of straw hats for summer. Am I a fop? What are my options?

Straw is a great material for summer wear because it's light and it breathes. There are dozens of options, from folky, rural Third World sombreros to finely woven panamas that can cost as much as a car, to the traditional English boaters and skimmers. The ultimate straw hat is the Montecristi, all woven in one town in Ecuador; the quality is amazing, and with proper care the hat should last as long as you do. It's fine enough to wear in the city with a summer suit, but it also offers you enough brim to wear for UV shielding on the beach. Other handsome panamas can be had for much less.

I also have a variety of funky, craftperson-made straws picked up around the Caribbean. They work on the beach, in the garden, or for funkier occasions. The classic boaters and skimmers require a certain amount of attitude to carry off properly. If you're a fop, you'll have no trouble with them. If you're not, you should at least have an arsenal of sharp retorts or martial arts at your command. Originally intended for boating, they came into fashion in the late nineteenth century. Later they often appeared in Hollywood films. Featured in Jimmy Cagney–type dance routines, these rigid, flat-brimmed, flat-topped hats have a broad ribbon around the crown. The boater has the smaller brim. You still see them on sharply dressed older guys in the summer, and they can work for young guys with that rare combination of elegance and balls. The skimmer is basically the same design with a broad brim. Boaters are fairly wind resistant; skimmers are probably so named because a good wind might cause them to skim across the water. They are relatively unsinkable.

What's a hip hat to wear this winter?

If you wear suits and traditional clothing, you can wear a traditional men's felt hat. The only problem is that a fedora or a porkpie doesn't keep your ears warm. Some wool golf-style caps, usually made in Scotland, have an earflap that folds down for brisk weather. Ski hats usually look dumb with suits and overcoats. Fur hats look . . . furry. I have a brown-and-gold Jamaican wool tam that can be worn covering my ears or not. It looks surprisingly good with my tobacco-colored cashmere overcoat, and it's natty and it's dread. And good Nixon masks are still available.

Are earmuffs too much with an overcoat and suit?

Too much? No. Not enough? Maybe. Instead of a hat? Okay, but most of your body heat escapes through the crown of your head. Are you afraid of hat hair? If your hairdo is too elaborate for head-gear, it may just be too elaborate. Earmuffs are better than nothing. Knitted ski bands spare the hair, and they don't look too stupid, unless you're dressed up. Black tie and black ski band? Might be funny enough to work.

What's the best way to clean a felt hat?

Send it to a hat cleaner. It's not expensive and life is too short.

Foul-Weather Guys

"The rain, it raineth on the just
And also on the unjust fella:
But chiefly on the just, because
The unjust steals the just's umbrella."

—Lord Bowen

I never liked the Boy Scouts much, but I always dug the slogan "Be prepared." It can be nasty out there, and there's nothing that looks more schmucky than a guy who's not dressed for the weather—guys in suits and low-vamp loafers, without hats, running through the rain under newspapers. I remember during the great New York Blizzard of 1982 seeing guys in parkas on snowshoes walking up Park Avenue, and thinking, "Now, that's cool."

Being cool involves being ready for rain, sleet, and snow. It means being windproof and ice resistant. It involves being able to master the elements and not being victimized by them.

It looks like rain. What should I do?

Some people, like me, love being out in it. This means raincoat, hat, proper footwear, and umbrella. Umbrellas are a difficult purchase because the cheap ones get blown away or destroyed by wind, often within minutes of purchase. Expensive ones are often left in taxis, restaurants, or wherever things can be lost. So I try never to pay too much for an umbrella or too little. Having one umbrella is something Noah wouldn't approve of. I believe in having an arsenal of umbrellas, sitting in a decorative umbrella container by the front door, including a few fairly fancy and sturdy umbrellas as well as a collection, found or bought impromptu on the street, of small Knirps-type folding umbrellas and economy umbrellas. This way if a friend shows up and decides to leave in a downpour, I can provide moving shelter and not care too much if it's ever returned. Also, in my golf bag and in the trunk of my car, there's always at least one fiberglass-shaft golf umbrella, excellent for walking two to one umbrella, and—this is important in the country—they're unattractive to lightning.

Raincoats are a matter of taste. I've tried on dozens of trench coats but never pulled the trigger. I thought they looked too theatrical or Sherlockian on me, but on some guys that look works. I like the classic Burberry-style khaki raincoat. It should come down to at least the bottom of the knee. Sometimes you encounter nice vintage raincoats in resale shops or at flea markets. I have a great iridescent one, slightly gold, but not far from the khaki classic. Black is also okay for a raincoat, especially for evening. If you can afford two, go for khaki and black. A nice feature on a raincoat is slits in the side pockets that allow you to put your hands into your jacket or trouser pockets without unbuttoning or lifting the coat. I've had rubber raincoats, and I loved them at first, but on a warm day it's like wearing a steam room. Also I find after a few hot summers they tend to melt in the closet, sticking to themselves. There are also canvas and rubber coats, an English specialty preferred by riders. These often have buttons up the side so you can adjust for being on horseback. I find this adjustment also works great for New York taxicabs. The traditional British mackintosh is also eternally groovy, but made of rubberized fabric, it can be hot if the weather isn't quite cool.

For less formal rainy days, or days where you'll engage in outdoor activities during precipitation, there's the miracle of Gore-Tex, a great synthetic microfiber that keeps you dry but breathes so you don't achieve saunalike body temperatures. Gore-Tex is what all the best golf rain suits are made of. You can play eighteen holes in a downpour and come back with dry undies. These suits are also great for rainy-day croquet, gardening, touch football, or what have you.

Rain footwear is important, as the worst part of getting wet is squishy shoes and socks. There are plenty of water-resistant shoes out there, and some shoes can be additionally waterproofed. When it pours I either go for the Timberland boots or my trusty rubber knee-high Wellington boots. Both of these will not only keep your piggies dry, they have enough tread to keep you out of most skids. They're like radials for your feet.

I can't afford a nice overcoat. Do I get a secondhand one or just go without?

Nothing wrong with secondhand, if you can find a good one. Or check for outlet stores in your area. Or make friends with a check-room attendant. Somewhere out there is an inebriated attorney celebrating the foreclosure of a poor family's mortgage and wearing a coat that would look a lot better on you, son. Good luck.

I bought a shiny silver down parka last winter, but now every time I put it on, I feel like a dork. What should I do with it?

The first thing I would do is try to return it to the store where you bought it for a full refund. Tell them that the salesman told you the silver would acquire a nice tarnished patina, it hasn't, and you suspect it's not genuine sterling. If that doesn't work, mail it to the Salvation Army in Aspen.

Every time I buy an umbrella, I lose it. What does this mean?

Maybe it means someone else needed it more than you do. Maybe it means you're lost in space. Maybe it means that we should not be too attached to material things, and if you're going to lose something, an umbrella is one of the less serious and most recyclable things to lose.

I like the look of camel hair coats. Are they non-PC?

No, they are made from camel hair, not camel skin. The camel doesn't have to give up his life.

Clean, Well-Groomed Guys

"Hygiene: Must always be carefully maintained. Prevents illness, except when it causes it."

—Gustave Flaubert

"Well-groomed people are the real beauties. It doesn't matter what they're wearing or how much their jewelry costs or how much their clothes cost or how perfect their makeup is: if they're not clean, they're not beautiful."

—Andy Warhol

Most of the questions the Style Guy receives have to do with grooming. An amazing number of letters have to do with getting rid of bodily hair, and an astounding number of letters are concerned with the elimination or eradication of pubic hair. Who knew? I had no idea there was such a move toward pubic hairlessness.

Once, on a journalistic assignment, I stayed at a couples resort in the Caribbean where there was a nude beach. I was surprised to see the extraordinary variety of topiary pubic hair treatments. I guess it's part of being a swinger.

Pubic hair, like head hair, is subject to fashion. When I was a boy trying to buy *Playboy* inside a *Life* magazine, the Playmates all had real bushes down there. Today they have token shrubbery, some so small they're like pubic Hitler mustaches. Being a moderate, I like a gal with a nice bikini wax, but I find baldness a bit on the pedophilic tip. Still, different strokes for different folks. It's a matter of personal taste. Maybe this below-the-waist shaving business just mirrors the trend toward shaved heads on men. I wonder if Mike's as slick below as he is above.

There is also a huge concern over zits and ingrown hairs.

Style Guy is not a Medical Guy, so we do the best we can. Eat well. Keep clean. Try that doctor's soap Phisohex on your little red bumps. Don't be afraid to use treatment products such as facial scrubs, toners, astringents, or masks. Using them doesn't make you feminine, it makes you aware of your skin. Many more women are aware of their skin than men are, but that doesn't mean we can't learn a thing or two from what they do.

Cleanliness and good grooming are essential to being attractive, stylish, and sometimes successful. You might not be able to afford a killer wardrobe, but if you're in good shape and clean and well groomed, you can still show that you have what it takes. It's a matter of pride, a matter of taste, and a crucial element in functioning as a babe magnet.

I have the back of an ape. Wax? Electrolysis? Nair?

Electrolysis would be impractical over such a large area. Waxing works well, and will make you smooth as a baby's heinie, but it can be painful. You might want to have a couple of margaritas before visiting the local beauty salon. (You can't do this alone, and professional help is highly recommended.) The Style Guy once had his back waxed researching an article for a women's magazine. I think the women editors wanted to see a guy suffering for beauty like women do. It hurt like a motherwaxer. I also got ingrown hairs, and my back was stripped by the top waxer to society ladies in New York City, the one with the German accent who laughed when I winced. Aside from pain, another downside is ingrown hairs, which can be nasty. But a waxing will last months, and after a few waxings the hair will probably come in much lighter. I don't know about the chemical depilatory Nair. I'm going to wait to see what happens to the first few generations of Nair users before I try it myself. If you really want to get rid of your fur permanently, there's a new laser process that gets rid of it forever. It gives the same results as electrolysis, but it's a lot quicker. (For information on what they call SoftLight, contact the American Dermatology Center, 210 Central Park South, New York, NY 10019, 212-247-1700.)

I have too much hair on my legs, and I hate it. What can I do?

It's probably a problem of length, not density. The kind of electric clippers that can be adjusted to give variable lengths—a crew-cut or goatee machine—can trim the excess from your legs. Or you could use scissors and a comb to take off the top.

I shave my chest. I don't have the funds for a wax job, and I'm starting to get ingrown hairs on my chest. How can I prevent them? Should I spring for the wax job?

Waxing won't prevent ingrown hairs. But if you're going for total aerodynamic smoothness, you might have to suffer through a few ingrowns. Style Guy thinks the swimmer, bodybuilder look is a little extreme (and preadolescent), so he just prunes the chest bush with scissors to avoid the Sasquatch-on-the-beach look.

There's a great product called Tend Skin, which helps ingrown hairs and razor burn or bumps. You should use it regularly if you have an ingrown-hair problem. You can find it in better drugstores. If you can't find a better drugstore, call Tend Skin at 800-940-8423. You can also fight ingrown hairs by using a scrubber—like a loofah, a scrub brush, or a bath mitt—in the shower and scrubbing, not till you draw blood but until the area is stimulated.

My face is a mess from shaving. It's flaky and I get red spots. It's only where I shave. I use an aftershave lotion, but it doesn't help.

It might hurt. A lot of guys like that bracing sting from aftershaves, but that alcohol isn't great for your face. It dries it out. What most men should really use after shaving is a moisturizer. Kiehl's makes a good one. So does Geo. F. Trumper of London. Check your better department stores. Also, one of the leading causes of razor bumps is using a dull blade. I know blades are expensive, but, hey, it's your throat.

What do you feel is the best type of fragrance for guys?

Odorless. Although I always thought my grandfather smelled manly in bay rum. Actually this is a really personal issue. I'm not a big fan of fragrance on men unless it's very subtle—that is, indistinguishable from a normal distance away. If a man's scent fills the elevator, he's wearing way too much. Style Guy often gets fragrances as gifts or payoffs, and they generally go unused, although he may consider "regifting" them to not-too-close giftees. On top of the list is anything containing musk or advertised as containing pheromones. More acceptable are the traditional citrus, bay rum, or spice colognes. Florals can be a problem. Style Guy was once stung by bees when wearing Chanel's Égoïste on the golf course. Style Guy has no problem with CK One and has been known to go transsexual when it comes to fragrance, having on occasions worn l'Eau d'Issey, Route de Thé, or L'Occitane's Concrete de Parfum (solid, not liquid) Vanille Bourbon. Say what you want, that doesn't make me a drag queen, men. By the way, one of the best-kept fragrance secrets in the world is Acqua di Parma, what Cary Grant smelled like.

I've always been advised that facial hair isn't a good idea for a job interview. Is a goatee acceptable, or should I shave for better results?

My grandfather would never hire a man with a mustache or beard, believing that he had something to hide. That's old-fashioned, but there are still plenty of employers out there who feel that way. Acceptability depends on what job you're applying for. If it's a creative job in an ad agency, you might be okay with a goatee. But if you're applying for a sales or account exec job, you'd better lose the chin whiskers. A goatee is not going to help you land any job, unless they're doing a remake of *Dobie Gillis* or *Gilligan's Island*, so why not go clean shaven until you're situated and see what the vibe is.

Many hair-removal products do not recommend using them near the family jewels. I am looking for a product or technique that will remove hair from the genital area. Razors are too dangerous around the testicles and the shaft of the penis. Can you recommend something?

Unless you have an unusually hirsute Johnson and basket, I'd suggest you use tweezers on your shaft and scrotum. Waxing works on pubic hair. It's not the most pleasant experience, but beauty can be painful.

Is it acceptable for males to pluck or shape their eyebrows? If so, how do you shape them?

Acceptable. Sometimes it's urgent. If it weren't for tweezers, there would be a lot of unibrows out there. Style Guy cuts his brows with scissors when they get too long, so as to avoid confusion with Soviet politburo members. If you start slow, plucking one or two hairs at a time, you can probably do it yourself. If you're unsure and your barber doesn't look like he moonlights doing Barbra or Judy impressions, maybe he can help you.

I've been plucking my eyebrows for two years. Now I can't stop or else I'll have huge, deformed bushes over my eyes. What can I do?

If you stop, your eyebrows won't be any bushier than before. That shaving and/or plucking encourages hair growth is an old ex-wives tale. In fact, after plucking and/or waxing, brows will grow in less heavily than before. That's why my grandmother had to draw her eyebrows on. (I guess you can blame Jean Harlow or Marlene Dietrich.) When you stop, your brows will gradually fill in to what they were before at the very best. Maybe they won't ever come back to the same fullness. Maybe you have judged them a little harshly. Bushy eyebrows can be attractive, distinguished, and gestural. Look at Fred MacMurray, John Lurie, Montgomery Clift. The great novelist Gabriel García Márquez has furry eyebrows as gigantic as the ones Groucho Marx drew on, and he's doing fine. Learn to raise one eyebrow at a time. Learn to raise both at once, rhythmically. You may discover that prominent eyebrows are the semaphore flags of the wit.

I have gray in my goatee, and I'd like it to disappear. I've tried over-the-counter dyes, but they really irritate my face. What's the answer?

Henna is a natural dye that's less irritating than many synthetic dyes. Henna is usually red, but it also comes in other shades. If there's not much gray, a henna treatment might just make it look like you've got red highlights. The eminent hairstylist Gad Cohen tells me the real deal is an especially nonirritating dye called Bigen that has no harmful ingredients. It's available where better beauty products are sold. Just add water and brush those years away.

I have athlete's foot and I can't shake it. I use Lotrimin. Isn't that what doctors give you?

Lotrimin works but you have to be incredibly conscientious about it and it takes a while to kill those parasitic fungi. I suffer from tinea pedis myself, and I found Lamisil, now available over-the-counter, seems to kill the little suckers off for good. I have also noticed that my feet look a lot better since I've been using moisturizer on them. Before I go to sleep I put Weleda Wild Rose Body Oil on my dogs, and my feet look better than they have in years. Another good foot greaser is shea butter. It's so rich your feet will feel they belong to Magnum P.I.

Most department store colognes are too strong or perfumy for me. I'm looking for something nice that's not overpowering.

Try something citrus based. I don't like leathery colognes. Who wants to smell like a saddle? I'm also for avoiding anything musk based. Musk is extracted from the sex glands of deer and may not be a wise choice, especially with the danger of deer-tick-borne Lyme disease. Who wants to attract Bambi?

I have a problem with ingrown hairs on my knees. How can I prevent them?

This is a new one to me, but offhand I'd say to avoid tight pants and tight jeans and pray sitting down till they go away.

Nose hair! Trim or pluck?

Ouch. Nose hair should be plucked only if you are bound, gagged, and the tweezers are in the hands of a woman in spike heels and a rubber dress. Trimming is the painless course. There are scissors made especially for this purpose. They have blunt ends so you don't stab your nostrils. The Hammacher Schlemmer catalog (800-

543-3366) sells a nifty, easy-to-use battery-powered nose-hair trimmer guaranteed to spare those sensitive schnozzola tissues. Be warned, young bucks, the older you get, the gnarlier those nose hairs will get. And if you don't have them already, chances are the ears will start sprouting, too. Be prepared with the right tools for the job.

My best friend has really bad breath. I haven't got the nerve or the heart to say something about it. How can I help diplomatically?

Ask them about your breath. Say "I ate a bunch of garlic. Is my breath okay?" It might get them thinking in the right direction.

What's better for your nails, buffing or varnishing?

Why not save buffing and varnishing for your hardwood floors and simply wash your hands frequently with soap and water, using a nail brush after acquiring a load of subcutaneal manly grit. It's also best to keep your nails at a civilized length, unless you are a pimp, a pusher, or build ships in bottles, in which cases long pinkie nails are tools of the trade. As we discussed in an earlier chapter, a lot of non-cross-dressing young men are wearing nail polish these days, usually something black or blue or scary. I think the New York Dolls pioneered the glitter polish look. But I don't think you can say that any of these things are good for your nails. Going in the ocean is good for your nails. And eating gelatin is good for your nails. Jell-O shots may actually be good for your nails.

I'm a magnet for pet hair. Everybody else will look clean and I'm covered in it. What's the best way to get it off?

It could be what you're wearing. Often permanent-press-treated fabric acts like a lint magnet. Cat hair loves to jump on silk. But all you need is a roller lint remover. It's a roll of tape, sticky side out, on a handle. The ultimate in lint brushes. No man with a pet or even occasional dandruff should be without one.

Since about September I have had a problem with my underarms sweating like a fountain. I'm up to two undershirts a day. What should I do? Do I need stress medication or a better deodorant?

Maybe you should ask a doctor. Some medications, like antidepressants, can cause excessive sweating. September? Sounds like it could be school induced. Nervous perspiration is the only kind that smells really bad. If you smell bad, it's probably stress related. If it is stress related, better to deal with the stress than with the armpits. You don't want cool, dry armpits and a bleeding ulcer.

I'm a profuse perspirer. I use deodorant, and my T-shirts and even my shirts develop bad yellow stains. What's up with this? How can I avoid them? How can I get rid of them?

Try avoiding deodorants with aluminum salts in them. These cause stains and they may not be good for you. Some researchers theorize that airborne aluminum, such as aerosol deodorants containing aluminum, might be a factor in Alzheimer's disease. They definitely will stain your clothes, if not your brain. As for existing stains, if bleach won't fix your T-shirts, buy some bluing and soak your T-shirts for a few hours in a basin with bluing, following the instructions. This will remove stains that bleach won't.

I have very sweaty armpits. I've tried every antiperspirant out there, and none of them seem to work. By the end of the day I'm left trying hide the sweat stains under my armpits at work. What can I do?

Wearing a T-shirt should help, absorbing sweat and giving it a chance to evaporate. I'm against antiperspirants. Nervous perspiration is bad because it smells like fear. The best cure for this type is to cure your nervousness. Try acting lessons or quitting your job. On the other hand, you might try the deodorant from Arm & Hammer baking soda. It's supposed to do a good job on heavy-duty armpits. *Details* editor David Keeps recommends Mitchum, which he claims gives your armpits aluminum (chlorohydrate) siding.

By the way, many readers have asked about a deodorant I recommend—Weleda all-natural sage. Sold in any good health food store. Brisk and bracing on the armpits. Smells nice and definitely won't give you Alzheimer's. Weleda also makes a nice citrus spray deodorant with no scary ingredients that's perfect for hot weather. It's not an antiperspirant, but it uses sage and other aromatic plant essences to make your pits pleasing. If you can't find it in a health food store or hip pharmacy, you can call 800-289-1969. By the way, all of these underarm sweat and odor problems can be helped somewhat by keeping underarm hair fairly neat. I'm not saying to shave the pits, but if you have a lot of hair, just prune it to a manageable level with a pair of scissors.

One day a few years ago I ran out of deodorant and substituted my wife's Secret. It worked great for me, and I've been using it ever since. Is this bad since it's pH balanced for a woman? My hair hasn't fallen out or anything, but I'm worried about the long-term effects it might have.

Remember *phooey* begins with *pH*. If it works and you're not having any problems now, I think you're quite safe. I think most deodorant doesn't know what sex you are. As long as it doesn't have estrogen in it, and it doesn't, you won't turn into a woman.

I know that the best time to spray cologne is after a hot shower, but where are the best places to spray it?

Hmm. Never heard of this hot-shower technique. I guess it makes sense, but I think you can feel free to spray whenever you feel like it. Just use discretion and don't become a one-man room deodorizer. They say the best places to apply fragrance are your pulse points, such as the wrists and throat. I wouldn't recommend the armpits as they're too sensitive to alcohol. On the rare occasions that I apply fragrance, I put a little dab between my collarbones just below my Adam's apple, and that dab does it for me.

I smoke and I use a breath freshener, but my main squeeze complains that my goatee makes kissing me taste like licking an ashtray. Help.

It seems like there are three choices. Quit smoking. Shave. Dump the squeeze. Which seems like the best idea?

My girlfriend has noticed that the area between my legs has a particularly funky odor, especially after I've been wearing pants all day. What do you recommend?

It sounds like you have two choices: Give up pants, or shower when you get home.

I love several designer male fragrances, but they seem expensive and they seem to last me only three weeks tops. Do you know something less expensive?

You're bathing in it, pal. You've got to cut back, if not for yourself, think of the neighbors. Just dab it on your pulse points, like your neck and wrists.

As for brands, when you're buying designer fragrances you're paying a lot for advertising. You can try designer knockoff fragrances, which are often advertised in sleazier men's magazines with names like *Butt Inspector* or *Jailbait Review*. They're at least similar to their inspiration, although the packaging won't impress anyone who detects your stash. Lots of designers have lesser-priced brands, like CK One, that are reasonable. Or you can go with an old standby like bay rum, a manly aroma I must say, or the old standby Lilac Vegetal or Old Spice—and why the hell not? But recently published studies by smellologists suggest that nothing will magnetize those vixens like the smell of good ole Good & Plenty. No kidding.

I'm a nineteen-year-old bisexual male, and my sex life hasn't been so good lately. My man and my lady like me to strip for them, and I usually wear a G-string, so of course I shaved my butt. Now it's covered with razor bumps. How can I get rid of them, or at least prevent them?

Well, son . . . I guess one of the leading brands of depilatory, such as Neet or Nair, might help prevent those nasty bumps. Or see the ingrown-hair question. Or maybe you should just find a nice couple that likes you just the way you are.

After I work out I usually hit the sauna to seat out whatever "impurities" I haven't gotten rid of during my workout. But I wonder if leaning my head up against the hot wooden wall is going to damage my hair follicles and hasten balding. Any other sauna advice?

Or maybe overheat your imagination. Uh, I don't think so. But if it's a worry, why don't you either sit up straight or put a towel over your head or behind it as a cushion. It'll give you that John Starks goes Arab look. As far as other sauna advice, definitely sit on a towel unless you want to expose yourself to random bodily fluids, strangers' "impurities," and effluvia.

I have a boyfriend who chews tobacco. I think it has something to do with baseball. I think it's disgusting. I won't be seen with him when he's doing it, and I won't kiss him unless he brushes his teeth first. He says that it is perfectly acceptable. Who's right?

You are. When was the last time you saw a bar or hotel lobby with a spittoon? The man is living in another era, or at least a very rural, doomed culture. If he needs a fix that bad, suggest that he try Nicorette. It offers all the nicotine without the vile spitting.

Guys with Hair (or Not)

"Long hair is all very well if it hangs loosely on silk or velvet, but it somehow seems all wrong when it's supposed to offset some smelly sport shirt."

—Noël Coward

Scalping was not a custom started by the American Indians. It was an ancient Celtic or Scythian practice, and it emerged in North America during the Indian Wars when mercenary Native American warriors were given a bounty for each scalp they took in battle. But there's something extremely personal about hair. It's always growing, and it seems to symbolize our life force.

Who knows if that was the origin of the value we place on our manly hair? And was a bald scalp rewarded equally with a fine hirsute specimen?

The legend of Samson lives on. He was a superhero until Delilah sheared his locks and rendered him human. To Hendrix it was a freak flag. To hippies it was an expression of commitment to peace and love, at least till the cops started to go shaggy. To a true Rastafarian it is a symbol of his knowledge of the living God.

Hair is a personal and intimate thing. That's your DNA in there.

*My girlfriend insists on cutting my hair. I'm suffering stylistically.
I look like a stand-in for the Monkees. How can I get peace for my
head and keep it in bed?*

Sounds a little controlling, this gal pal of yours. The only valid
reason for her wanting to cut your hair is that she is a professional.
She may not like your hair the way you like it, but it is, after all,
your hair. Maybe you should ask her if she'd like you to help her
work her way through barber college. Or why not suggest that you
both cut each other's hair. That will probably get her to drop the
whole issue.

I was wondering if ponytails on men are fashionable these days?

We seem to be seeing them less, or at least seeing less of those
minitails sported by aging swingers. I think they'll always be acceptable for those of you with enough hair to warrant keeping it out of
your face with a ponytail. If your hair is too short, it looks like
you're an off-duty bond trader posing as a creative director.

*What's the best hairbrush for guys? (I'm Asian and have long,
straight hair.)*

The real question is, What's the best hairbrush for long, straight
hair? Your hair doesn't know it's on a guy. Most of the women
I know, who spend more time brushing than the guys I know,
swear by Mason Pearson brushes, which come in all shapes and
sizes. Since you have long, straight hair you probably want a flat
brush. A round brush will impart some curl. (Say, if you're going for
the Fabio look.) By the way, occasional brushing is good for
everyone, even short hairs. It pulls out the dead stuff and stimulates
the scalp. Most dogs love a good brushing, and dogs know what's
good.

I have brown hair. Summer's here and I want to go blond. But not all blond, just a kind of brushed-through look. How do I do it?

The safest way, both for looks and for hair health, is to go to a pro. If you really want to do it yourself, you have two choices. You can buy a frosting kit, probably in the women's hair section of your drugstore, and follow the directions, combing or painting it through where you want the highlights. Or, if you want to go safe and organic, mix equal parts lemon juice and chamomile tea, put it in a spray bottle, spray it where you want blondness, and then go enjoy the sunshine. It'll take a little longer, but it will look more natural and you won't be using chemicals in close proximity to your brain.

Help! I'm losing it. I don't think I can face baldness, but can I face wearing a rug? Plugs seem worse. Help!

Rogaine (minoxidil) seems to work for the Mailman, the buff Mr. Karl Malone, but a few of my friends swear by Propecia. It's by prescription only. Apparently 83 percent of the men who take it don't lose any more hair, although something like 2 percent of the men who take it suffer from a droopy libido as a side effect, but if that happens, all you have to do is stop. See your doctor. As for rugs, I don't think they've looked good on anybody but Andy Warhol and Joe Pesci in *JFK*. I think the best thing for most guys who are going irreversibly bald is to either shave your head or cut your hair very short. You can try to fool people an elaborate and expensive way, with transplants and such, or with toupees, or you can try cheapo, fool-yourself techniques like scalp dyes or the dreaded comb-over, but sooner or later somebody's going to run their fingers through your hair (or whoever's hair it is), and you'll be found out. Better to be caressed on your tanned and buffed scalp.

I'm twenty-two and I'm going bald already. I feel like I'm too young for Rogaine. Should I shave it like Andre Agassi?

Why too young for Rogaine? If you're going to use Rogaine or Propecia, you might as well try to nip your baldness in the root, huh? But Agassi looks cool, too.

I am twenty-four years old and cannot grow a mustache or a beard. It grows in thin and spotty. Is there anything I can do to make it grow in thick?

First of all, why do you want a beard or mustache? Is it because you can't have one? You might consider yourself lucky for not having to shave too often. Maybe Rogaine works for the face, but I wouldn't try it without first consulting a doctor.

I use a small amount of toothpaste to hold my hairstyle in place. Am I nuts?

Only if it rains. Or if you brush with Brylcreem.

I'm twenty years old. My hair is straight and dull, and I've been thinking of getting a perm in my hair. Is this a masculine thing to do?

Why the hell not? But if you're worried about being masculine, maybe you should call it a permanent wave instead of a perm. Before going that far you might try various combinations of shampoos, conditioners, and grooming gels. If you want more body in your hair, don't wash it too often.

My boyfriend is a really sweet, good-looking guy. I love everything about him except for his hair, which he hasn't changed since college. It's long with reddish highlights. I think he would look great with a shorter, more conservative do. He's intelligent and other-

wise has great taste. How can I suggest a change without hurting his feelings?

If he's good looking and intelligent, I don't think he'd mind your suggestion. Maybe he's trying to hold on to his youth. There comes a point in every guy's life when long hair doesn't look as good as it used to. Maybe he's getting there. But change is good, and if he doesn't like it, it will always grow back.

I'm in my early thirties, and I'm totally prematurely salt-and-pepper. It makes me feel old, but I don't want to dye my hair. Sometimes it looks dirty and yellow. How can I make the most of my unwanted silver?

Silver is good. Especially if you have a young face. It may help you get that pay raise. It can make you look like you've been around. The drag about gray hair is that it can look yellow, and yellow gray hair looks shabby. Better to go platinum blond or make sure that the silver stays. There are several shampoos, such as Shimmer Lights by Clairol, that are made for platinum blond and/or gray or white hair. They're intensely blue, and washing with them will take away the yellowness and replace it with ultraviolet steely magnetic intensity. Or something. But they'll make that senior hair look as good as a silver Porsche 911 Targa.

I'm a college student and weekend surfer. I really dig the Rasta look. I've seen white guys with dreads, but I'm not sure how you get them.

The main thing is not combing. The dread look is based on a passage in the Bible that instructs the followers of King David not to cut or comb their hair or shave their beards. Obviously some Rastafarians shave and cut their dreads, but basically it's a nonfashion look that became fashion. Don't wash too much. A lot of dreads wash their hair in salt water, which will give it extra body, then twist their hair into locks. Unfortunately this isn't going to work if you have really straight or limp hair. You might have to get a permanent first, seen?

I have bad dandruff. I've tried a lot of shampoos, but nothing seems to help much. What can I do besides avoiding black and navy blue?

Use a tar-based shampoo. I like T/Gel from Neutrogena because it's not too strong—that is, it won't leave you smelling like a brand-new road. Try a tar shampoo for a month, and if your dandruff isn't better, it's off to the dermatologist with you.

I've grown up a bit and gotten tired of my 1960s army cut, shaved on the sides, an inch on top. We don't have any fancy salons around here to offer advice. What can I do?

It sounds a little corny, but it works. Pick out a haircut you like from a magazine, such as *GQ, Details, Lowrider, L'Uomo Vogue, Custom Classic Trucks*, or *Martha Stewart Living*, and show it to your barber and tell him you want to go there. Tom Cruise, Dennis Rodman, Robert Downey, Jr. The girls seem to like that George Clooney look. I think he got it from a picture of me.

I'm twenty-seven and I have been growing my hair out, and now that it's longer I notice that if I run my fingers through it, especially in the shower, I get hairy palms. Am I going bald?

Not necessarily. Everybody loses lots of hair every day. If you notice it's thinning in a particular area, that's a sign of baldness, but hair attrition happens to everybody. You probably just didn't notice it when there wasn't enough to run your fingers through.

How much should I tip a hairstylist? Is it the customary 15 percent like in restaurants (unless the service is bad)?

Restaurant tipping is a good guideline. Ten percent for adequate service, 15 percent for good service, 20 percent for exceptional service. Of course, if they destroy your looks, don't tip. And if you go to a fancy salon and there's a shampoo person, they should get something, too (maybe $3).

Shaved heads are really catching on. How do you shave your head, and what's involved in keeping that smooth, clean-shaven "bald" look?

First you might want to closely inspect your noggin to make sure bald will work for you. I myself would make a horrifying baldhead because I have a big dent in the back of my skull and a fairly glaring purple birthmark. But assuming your head is fair and shapely, you can shave it the same way you shave your face, with blade or electrically. There's no particular technique, but you can watch how Mr. Jordan shaves his in his recent cologne commercial. If you've never exposed your pate to the elements before, be sure to wear some sunscreen, and you may want to use a little moisturizer up there. What's worse than a bald guy with dandruff?

I recently shaved my head. The hair is growing back now, and it's about an inch long. Unfortunately it's growing back crooked. Should I shave it again? Are shaved heads in fashion?

As long as Michael Jordan and Charles Barkley (and Matt Geiger) are around, shaved heads will have their appeal. As far as retraining your reemergent locks, try shaping your do with a hair cream that's not too greasy but doesn't harden (like Clairol's Vitapointe or Kiehl's Silk Groom). Your look should be back under your control in no time.

I'm getting out of the military, and I plan to grow my hair out. What is considered too long in the civilian job market?

This varies greatly depending on the job. In heavy industry it's a good idea to wear it short enough so that it doesn't get caught in the machinery. In most offices I think that as a rule, if it's long enough that a ponytail doesn't look ridiculous, it's too long. If you're in the creative department at an ad agency, it should probably be shorter than Charles Manson's.

What is the best shampoo for a man's hair?

I think the concept of a man's shampoo, like that of a man's soap, man's deodorant, or man's hair dye, is really more about feeling manly than actual performance. Hair is hair. Women are more likely to have damaged hair because more of them bleach and perm, and damaged hair needs special care. Instead of thinking about gender-specific shampoo, think about whether your hair is thick or thin, dry, regular, or oily. You'll find plenty of shampoos and conditioners specifically formulated for these hair types. It's a good idea, no matter what shampoo you like, to use Neutrogena shampoo once in a while. It gets rid of shampoo residue that builds up from your regular brand. Oh, and it's okay for a man to use a conditioner. It's not unbutch, okay?

I was wondering if styling gel and hair products promote hair loss, and if so, what products are more dangerous to the hairline?

Virtually all styling products, shampoos, and conditioners are completely safe for your hair and scalp and won't cause hair loss. Almost all hair loss comes from your genes, not what you put on your hair. You can, however, damage your hair—usually this is a result of frequent bleaching. If you have damaged hair, there are plenty of excellent conditioners and treatment products that will help it out.

I would like to get a new haircut for spring break vacation. Can you recommend any new styles?

That's kind of a tough one. But the other night I was watching a jazz documentary on PBS, and there was the great tenor saxophonist Sonny Rollins, probably in the mid sixties, wearing a Mohawk. At the peak of his career Sonny Rollins, one of the great sax men of all time, took a year off to practice by himself on the Williamsburg Bridge, high above the East River in New York City. It was probably not long after returning to performing that Sonny briefly adopted the Mohawk. I prefer to think of it as a Mohican. Why not try a Mohican this spring break? Sonny Rollins, Henry Rollins, and John Riggins can't all be wrong.

My dad has a comb-over, which I find really embarrassing. If my genes destine me for baldness, I'll shave myself totally bald before I comb over. What do you think?

The good news is that supposedly baldness is inherited from the maternal side. How's your mother's father's hairline? It's true that few things look worse than an extreme comb-over. I guess a really bad rug is worse. A friend of mine had a great term for the comb-over. He called it *moving the suburbs to Paris*. I have always found the most effective tactic to be wearing whatever's left short and being balding and proud. In the initial stages minor combing over combined with minoxidil or Propecia will hold the fort for a while. But sooner or later you might as well go public. I don't think baldness is such a big deal. It seems to be working fine for the likes of Michael Stipe, Billy Corgan, and half of the NBA. It's trying to hold on to what you ain't got that's unattractive.

Polite Modern Guys

"Proper words in proper places, make the true definition of a style."

—Jonathan Swift

've noticed lately that when I invite people to dinner parties they say "Maybe." This is not good. Some people blame it on television, Hollywood films, bad parenting. I think you can put the blame for rudeness only on the rude person themselves. You may have grown up among apes, but if you're smart, you can still pick up on the social contract, baby.

In what circumstances is using a cellular phone just too gauche for words?

In movies or at plays, at a restaurant (unless you're alone), in a business meeting, on a golf course, or on a date. Anywhere where a sudden ringing will disturb others or cause others annoyance at the interruption and diversion of your attention. I recently attended a funeral where four cellular phones rang during the service. My Motorola StarTAC phone can be set on vibrate only, so it doesn't ring and bother other diners. The new Nokia features caller ID so you can make a good guess whether it's an urgent call or not. The above guidelines also apply to beepers.

I let the generic computer voice answer my answering machine. Is this uncool? She sounds better than I do most of the time.

I'd rather her, the computer-chip woman, than a dumb musical interlude or bad jokes. The only problem is that sometimes you'll confuse callers, and they may call again just to make sure that they've dialed the right number.

A friend of mine has his secretary place all of his phone calls. I find this truly annoying, especially when it's a personal call. Is he putting on airs?

You bet. Most of the really important people I know make their own calls. And we know that the president makes his own phone calls, at least to his subordinate intimates. How much longer does it take to do it yourself? I sometimes have my assistant place a call, but I'll yell "Let me know when it's ringing," and pick it up before they do. It's a matter of courtesy. It means I think your time is just as important as mine. A self-important painter of my acquaintance once had his secretary get me on the line first; after I waited for a minute or two he came on the line. "Glenn?" he said. "Please hold for Mr. O'Brien," I said, holding my nose for my best Lily Tomlin as Ernestine, the telephone operator, voice. Thick as he is, I'm sure he got the point.

My mother taught me that I should open the car door for a female. I find that most of my dates do it for themselves automatically. Who's right?

Most modern women do it themselves. On a first date you might make a gesture. And it's always a good move if you're going somewhere where a major gown is involved. It can't hurt. But, as you say, most modern women do it themselves, but they also probably appreciate the gesture.

A man and a woman are about to get in a cab. Who gets in first? Should he get in first, since it's more work to slide over?

Good question. I don't know how Miss Manners or Emily Post feel, but I feel like it's often a courtesy for the guy to get in first, depending on what she's wearing. But since this goes against the old ladies-first dictum, I find myself usually prefacing this action with, "I'll get in first," or "Shall I get in first?" thereby informing the young lady that I'm not a boor. When it comes to lifeboats, however, it's polite to let the lady get in first and slide over.

I'm a young lawyer. When I go to parties people are always hitting me up for free legal advice. I hate it. What's the best way to handle this?

Well, you could ask for their name and address and send them a bill the next day. You could ask them what they do and try to swing a barter deal. Or just give them your business card and tell them that you'd love to help them, call you at the office. They'll probably get the idea that business conducted in the office gets billed.

My best friend and I got into a stupid argument at school, and now we haven't spoken for nine months. I don't think it was my fault, but I feel stupid. I don't want to lose her as a friend. What do I do?

See, you can't even remember what started it. When I get in situations like this I just remember my two favorite words in the auto insurance business: No Fault! Half the time stupid arguments like this can be consigned to the no-fault pile. Just tell your friend that you miss her and that if you offended her, you're sorry. Tell her you want to forget the whole thing and see if you can start over. If that doesn't work, try a little gift. If she insists on placing blame, accept it this one time, but don't make a habit of it. She could be a chronic blamer, and blame, like a beautiful sunset, is best when shared.

A good friend of mine stands too close to people when he talks. He's normal in every other way, but this makes me and others uncomfortable. What's he thinking about, and how can I let him know it makes me uncomfortable?

A lot of the distance issue, like the touching issue, is cultural and regional. Maybe your friend is from someplace where everyone stands at that distance when talking. Or maybe he's hard of hearing. Have you tried taking a step backward? Does he then advance toward you? Have you tried saying "Shall we dance?" or "I can hear you fine." If he's a good friend, I think you could mention it diplomatically. Ask about it. "You know, you stand closer than most people. Did you know that?" Chances are his other friends won't be so direct, and if you say it in a really sincere and friendly way, you may be helping him out.

I asked a professional athlete for an autograph in a restaurant. He gave it to me, but my girlfriend was mortified. Am I justified?

No. These days autographs are best obtained when the jock is getting paid at a card show or department store. Privacy is worth fighting for, even if it isn't yours. Autograph. Big deal. Wouldn't you rather have a sense of cool?

I was brought up to give my seat in public transportation to pregnant women, the elderly, and nuns. I've noticed that not many people do this anymore. Is it passé?

Not unless kindness, compassion, and good manners are passé, young man. Give up that seat. But I wouldn't give my seat to a nun unless she was also elderly or pregnant.

My girlfriend says that when we're invited to dinner we should send a thank-you note. This seems stupid to me. Who's right?

She is, stupid. People just don't send enough thank-you notes. Thank-you notes should be sent at the drop of a hat. Even if it's just "thanks" scrawled on the back of a postcard of the Grand Canyon. People love to be thanked in writing. You would, too, I bet.

I'm always late. Is there a good excuse?

No.

I've got a black-tie-optional wedding to go to. I figure the only guys in tuxes will be groomsmen, and I don't even have a suit. Should I rent a tux, buy a suit, or find a nice jacket?

You are now faced with the first step in adult dressing. Forget renting the tux. It's probably time for you to buy your first suit, or maybe a navy blazer. A suit is probably your best bet. Navy blue or charcoal gray would be versatile options. You're going to be going to a lot more weddings (not to mention funerals), so even if you never work a day in your life in a suit, it will still come in handy. But go for something conservative. That way you'll be ready for any occasion.

When I valet-park my car, is it customary to tip both the valet who parks it and the valet who brings it back, or just when it comes back?

I'd recommend a dollar each way. It's the cheapest insurance policy you'll ever get.

I usually use a full-service gas station in my neighborhood, and the attendants usually wash the car windows without me asking. Last week I was chatting with one of them. He asked me if I wanted my windows done, and when I left I tipped him a few bucks. Should I always tip them?

Maybe you should look for a new gas station. Full-service pumps usually cost more than self-service. Presumably the difference is to cover the, yes, "full service." If you enjoy tipping, then, okay, but it's not necessary; you've already paid for it.

I find a lot of answering machine messages annoying. Am I overly cranky?

Maybe not. A lot of answering machines are truly annoying, particularly ones that go on forever. It's okay to be a little funny, as long as you fit it in, say, four seconds. People know to leave a message. They might want to hear the number, so they'll know they've reached the right one. Instructions on how to send you a fax are appropriate, or how to beep you or reach you on your mobile (if you really want to broadcast your mobile number). But generally, long, trying-too-hard-to-entertain messages are obnoxious. Worse than being put on hold to a Kenny G solo.

I hate it when I go to the doctor or the dentist and they say, "Hello, John, I'm Dr. Smith." Am I being overly sensitive?

Nope. This is but one of the ways doctors try to make you feel vulnerable, and more likely to be kept waiting for an hour without complaining. If a doctor wants to be called Dr. Smith, he should call you Mr. Doe, no? My doctor calls me Glenn and I call him Steve and it's more civilized. I have yet to bring up the matter of deducting waiting time from his fee, however.

This question has caused a lot of debate at my school. We're required to wear name tags to some events, and one's natural inclination is to affix it to one's left lapel. A certain dean insists that it's proper to wear one's name tag over the right lapel so it's easier to read when shaking hands. Who's right?

Nobody. I say, wear the damn thing wherever you want. Or don't wear it and tell the dean you know your name. How about wearing it on your fly? Or why not trade name tags with your friends. I was Max Blagg the other night at a fund-raiser and it was fun. If you insist on playing it straight, however, I'd say the military must have some reason for wearing it on the left breast, over the heart. At ease, men.

Recently I find myself in conversations where people make inquiries that make me feel uncomfortable. Questions about my finances or my sex life. How much rent do I pay. I was brought up to believe that it was rude to discuss money, politics, religion, and sex with casual acquaintances. Is there a polite way of saying "Fuck off"?

"There's the door. What's your hurry?" "I beg your pardon!" Or when they ask how much rent you pay, you can always say "I own." You might try laughing and changing the subject. The chances are that these rude people know better, they just want to see how far they can push you. I don't like people I'm paired up with on the golf course asking me what I do, so if they ask, I usually tell them I work at McDonald's and they drop it. "You don't want to know" is also a very good answer, particularly if they have the gall to ask you about your sex life.

I know the image of the cigarette smoker used to be rebellious and the image of the cigar smoker is the trendy, tycoon type. I've recently picked up the habit of smoking clove cigarettes. What's our image thus far?

Stinky.

I have a memory like a sieve. I often forget the names of people I know, even those I know fairly well. The pressure of introducing people at parties seems to cause me to panic, and it makes it even worse. What can I do?

I have troubles like this sometimes. So I try to use mnemonic devices to remember their names—a trick to help remind you. Say you know someone named Lois Marino; just think Superman Dolphin. I know it sounds dumb, but it actually works. And if you can't remember, just say "I'm so sorry. I've forgotten your name." It happens to everybody and they're used to it, and most people would prefer the direct approach.

A friend insists that the correct way to eat a sandwich, especially in a posh restaurant, is with a knife and fork. I insist that eating a sandwich with your hands is correct everywhere.

I'm with you. Unless we're talking open-faced hot roast beef, turkey with gravy, an overstuffed sauce-dripping meatball hero, or something generally unwieldy and dripping. Of course, you should wash your hands before gripping a sandwich.

What is the best way to blow your nose in public?

If you absolutely have to, in a handkerchief, as far away from other people as possible, hopefully among strangers or people you detest. That's what hankies are for. The same rules apply to crying in public.

What is the best way to avoid having dinner with a professional colleague?

Just say no.

Guys and Guys?

"It is in this century misunderstood, so much misunderstood that it may be described as the Love that dare not speak its name, and on account of it I am placed where I am now. It is beautiful, it is fine, it is the noblest form of affection. There is nothing unnatural about it … The world mocks at it and sometimes puts one in the pillory for it."

—Oscar Wilde, from his trial transcript

Times have changed. Gay love is no longer what, in the time of Oscar Wilde, was "the Love that dare not speak its name." Today it's more likely to be the love that likes to shout its name. That's what happens when you dare not speak for centuries. Suddenly you've got a lot to say.

Many of the questions on relationships and dating that are covered in "Guys and Girls" apply equally to guys and guys. Relationship issues are generally about respect and kindness and understanding, and such things are not usually gender based. Actually guys may have an easier time relating to other guys' feelings.

Times are changing, and every year more and more Americans have a gay friend. Even though there are plenty of people out there determined to "cure" gay people, through religion or "Aesthetic Realism" or analysis, more and more people are beginning to understand that gay people are like everybody else, just a little different. But we're still in a period of transition, so situations are bound to arise that cause conflict and bad feelings. The answer, ironically, is a little more "Christian charity" from everyone.

I know it is proper to light a cigarette for a woman, but what about another guy? My friends and I are debating this. I think it's best to hand the guy the lighter and let him light his own cigarette.

I sometimes do that on the golf course if the wind is over twenty miles per hour, but in ordinary social situations I'm happy to light my friends' coffin nails, and oddly enough, it never occurred to me that there was anything suggestive about it. By the way, it's very bad to light a cigarette from a candle. The wax is worse for you than anything the government is warning you against in the tobacco. It is also very bad to put a cigarette or cigar down on the grass on the golf course and then pick it up and smoke it again. Burning pesticides suddenly coursing through the bloodstream, baby!

I'm new to the gay scene. I've noticed that guys wear different-colored handkerchiefs in their back pockets to indicate certain preferences. Can you tell me what they mean?

No. It's sock colors that have different meanings, and I'm not allowed to say.

My best friend from school recently introduced me to his new boyfriend Gary. (I'm straight.) Gary made a pass at me, which is cool with me, but should I tell my best friend?

It might be better to just forget about it. The truth isn't going to make anybody happier. But if you're going to bring it up, the best way might be to do so in a good-natured way when you're with both of them.

My friend and I had a huge argument over whether or not it's a fashion faux pas for close friends or a couple to wear the same article of clothing together.

Whenever I see a couple dressed alike, it gives me the creeps. I don't care if they're married, gay life partners, boyfriend and girlfriend, boyfriend and boyfriend, girlfriend and girlfriend, or twins. Twins especially should be encouraged to not coordinate or even clash. Dressing is about individuality, unless you're going for a uniform look or a fetish thing. It always gives me pause to see a gay couple that looks too much alike. Cloning is so narcissist. I guess it's fine for dating cops or married mail persons or cruising leather boys, but variety is the spice of life, baby.

Being a modern guy, I sometimes grab a drink with my gay business associates at their local hangout. What's the nicest way to deal with a guy when he offers to buy me a drink?

Accept it. It's only a drink, Mary.

I just moved east from the midwest, and I've noticed that guys around here often greet each other with a kiss on the cheek. And I mean straight guys. This makes me feel weird. What should I do?

Just stick your hand out a little farther than you otherwise might. Cheeky kissing is often found in New York, or in L.A. for that matter. It's not a sign of latent lust. It doesn't mean anything except "I feel European" or "I'm not hung up." It's okay. You'll get used to it. Kiss kiss.

My parents are coming to visit, and I'm very friendly with my next-door neighbors, a gay couple. How do I introduce them to my parents?

Mom, Dad, this is Bill and Bob. You don't have to spell out their relationship, even though you've spelled out your parents. Actually, instead of Mom and Dad, use their names. Phyllis, Fred, meet Bill and Bob. That way they'll have something to call your folks other than Mom and Dad.

I have two very good friends who are a gay couple. I really enjoy the time we spend together, but sometimes they hold hands in public or kiss and it really bugs me. Am I a hypocrite?

Style Guy doesn't particularly like to see heterosexual couples kissing in public. Especially in Paris. It makes him jealous. I'm no Muslim fundamentalist, but I think that discretion is a part of intimacy. There will always be public displays of affection, and a little hand holding isn't going to hurt anyone. (Which is not to say that there aren't places where guys holding hands might get hurt.) If such a simple gesture offends people—and if it were two teenage girls, it surely wouldn't—then maybe they need to grow up and accept the realities of human nature.

What's a good gift for a lesbian couple?

Towels that say "Hers" and "Hers."

Drinking Guys

"Knowledge is seldom lacking in the degree that will is lacking."

—Ezra Pound

"Drunk: Always preceded by the word roaring."

—Gustave Flaubert, *The Dictionary of Received Ideas*

M en drink. Or they don't drink. But either way they have to have a policy, a code of conduct that they can live well with. It's all the difference between a raconteur and a loudmouth, the life of the party or the guy with the lampshade on his head. Some guys can drink, some guys can't. The important thing is knowing which side of the line you're on.

If drinking changes your personality, it's probably not a good idea. You might not notice, but if your friends indicate that they partied with Mr. Hyde the night before, take heed.

Drinking beer out of the bottle—cool or uncouth?

Drinking beer out of the bottle is pretty accepted practice. It's certainly more culturally acceptable than swigging merlot out of a fifth or slogging down milk from a quart carton with the pictures of missing children on the side. But using a glass will always be more civilized than straight from the bottle or can. It's not just appearances. Good beer tastes better in a glass. A glass allows a head to develop and the aroma to reach your nose. Like wine, beer has bouquet. Different beers have different glassware. The Belgians, the world's most advanced beer drinkers, have a glass for every different style (and brand) of beer. It may be my imagination, but Delirium Tremens just seems to taste better in a big, snifterlike Delirium Tremens glass. And pilsner definitely seems to taste better in a long, conical pilsner glass. Native Irish have told me that drinking Guinness out of the bottle will give you a headache. It certainly doesn't compare to drinking it out of a proper pint glass where every sip leaves a ring of foam, enabling one to determine exactly how many swallows consumed the pint. I'm sure a 1978 Chateau Ducru Beaucaillou tastes pretty good out of a Flintstones 1978 jelly jar juice glass, but a nice crystal Bordeaux glass is one thing that separates us from the Piltdown man.

What's the etiquette of repo-ing my booze at the end of a party at someone else's house?

The only booze you can take with you politely is what's coursing through your bloodstream.

A friend of mine, who is charming and knowledgeable, makes a big deal out of ordering wine in restaurants. First he has to survey what everyone is having, and then he decides what to order. Sometimes he'll even try to get somebody to change their dinner order to suit his wine selection. What's up with this?

It's a little pretentious. It's true that certain wines complement certain dishes, but the whole white-with-fish, red-with-meat thing is a little old-fashioned. I think red goes fine with a full-flavored fish like salmon or tuna. And lots of people I know prefer drinking white with whatever in the summer, simply because the wine is cool and the weather is hot. Light red wines can also be chilled. The value of connoisseurship is to know when you're breaking the rules, not to stop you from breaking them.

I have a friend who routinely drinks too much. It's obvious, but he insists he's capable of driving home.

If you've tried reasoning over and over, try it again when he's sober. If that fails, have a good pickpocket around who could snatch the keys, make a show of looking for them, and then drive him home. (Make sure he doesn't block the driveway when he shows up.) Or you can unplug the distributor cap. That's easy and he won't think of it. But after it happens a few times, he might get the hint. Next time offer to pick him up on the way to the party.

How do you survive a brutal hangover on the job?

Does this mean you're planning on doing it again? If it becomes a habit, you'll have to stop partying on school nights, kiddo. Robert Benchley wrote, "The only cure for a really bad hangover is death." Aspirin works on the headache. So does coffee, but don't drink enough to give you the jitters. Cream in the coffee might upset your stomach. Breathing oxygen helps a lot, but it seems a little decadent (and possibly dangerous) to keep it around for such purposes. Some hoisters and swiggers swear by Emergency, a fizzy vitamin C and minerals concoction sold in most drugstores. Health-conscious dipsomaniacs often recommend Nux Vomica, a homeopathic hangover remedy. The classic cure is the "hair of the dog that bit you" (that's a hair, not the whole dog), but times have changed. If you are an executive, maybe you can get away with a Bloody Mary at lunch. If you operate heavy machinery, take the day off and avoid the Benchley cure.

I'm tired of Cosmopolitans and Sex on the Beach. What's a cool new summer cocktail?

The Goldeneye is served by Chris Blackwell at his Jamaican hacienda of the same name, the former estate of James Bond creator Ian Fleming. Take one jigger of Appleton Jamaica rum, one-half ounce lime juice, one-half ounce orange juice, one-half ounce pineapple juice, and a dash of cherry juice or grenadine for color. Shake well with ice or blend for a frozen version.

I've been to several restaurants that talk about corkage fees on the menu. Duh?

A corkage fee is the amount charged by the restaurant when you bring in your own bottle, they open it for you, give you some glasses, and let you drink it. It sounds pretentious, but if you're an oenophile—i.e., an expensive wino—this can be a blessing in pretentious disguise. Why? Most restaurants charge at least a 100 percent markup over retail on wines: ten bucks at the liquor store, twenty-plus at the table. So if a restaurant charges a $15 corkage fee, you're saving money on any bottle that you paid more than $15 for at the store. Not to mention tax and a 15 to 20 percent tip. Only problem is, you can't send it back.

Do you have any guidelines for ordering wine at a restaurant, besides price and the largely unknowledgeable wait staff, short of getting a degree in oenology?

If a restaurant doesn't have a knowledgeable wait staff, maybe you should stick with beer or cocktails there, because there's a good chance the wine list isn't worth it. Most restaurants with good wines educate their staff on the list. Ask them what they recommend. Chances are it will be okay, especially if it's not the least expensive thing on the list. You might ask at a knowledgeable wine store if they have a pocket vintage guide, so at least you'll know if it's a good year you're ordering. Chances are an '83 Bordeaux isn't going to suck. You can also get to know a few of the highly reputable major vintners and exporters. Chances are if it's a Mondavi or Beaulieu from California, or a Louis Jadot or Joseph Drouhin from France, it will range from very drinkable to excellent. But there's a whole world of wines out there. I'm very fond of the trial-and-error system in learning about it. And, of course, if it's really wretched, you can send it back.

I feel awkward with the whole ritual of ordering wine in a good restaurant. I usually say, "I'm sure it's okay," and let the waiter pour it. Am I being unpretentious or dumb?

Dumbish. You should always taste the wine, even if it's an expensive one in a great restaurant. Especially then. You might hate the whole ceremony, thinking it's pretentious—them presenting the label for you to read, handing you the cork, pouring a taste. But the fact is that a not-insubstantial percentage of wines go bad. Saying "I'm sure it's okay" might seem cool, but it's not all that smart. Wine is tasted because a small percentage of bottles, even in the best restaurants, are going to come up bad. If you drink wine regularly, sooner or later you're going to get a bad bottle. Merde happens, as they say in Bordeaux. You will detect a musty, corky odor or a vinegary taste. You won't like the stuff. You can still send it back, even if it has been poured, because nobody else is going to want to drink that bottle, but it's better to observe the ritual and take that little taste before it's poured all the way around. If you have any doubts about whether the bottle you're being offered is bad, ask the waiter or maître d' to try it. It's not good form, however, to send back a bottle just because you've made a poor choice and you don't like the style. You won't impress anyone if you send back a perfectly good bottle of wine. It's not a good idea to piss off people who are feeding you unless you want a fly in your soup.

Some bozos think it's impressive to their dates to send a bottle back. I went into one of my favorite Italian restaurants the night that the *New York Times* had run a piece on how to send back a bottle of wine. My friend Silvano, the owner, was fairly loaded. Several tables had sent back perfectly good bottles, and to prove them wrong, he drank them. But another night, same place, I sent back two bottles of the great Italian chardonnay Maculan because they were corked, and Silvano was with me all the way. (I'm sure he was prepared to drink them if I were wrong.) Anyway, the third had charm.

A friend of mine says that you shouldn't use vodka from the freezer to make martinis. Could this be true? I thought the colder the better.

True. To get the right martini mix, you want the vodka and vermouth to interact with the ice. If the vodka is too cold, the ice won't melt and you'll have a martini that's overproof. It will get you drunk, but it won't taste as good in the process.

I was with some friends and working associates at a bar. We were buying rounds, and when it was the last guy's turn to buy he said he had enough and didn't take his turn. What do I do next time?

Next time he should buy the first round. Or you could try paying for your own drinks. This is often the best policy for young tipplers on a budget.

How do you get the beer smell out of sofas and rugs?

It depends on how the smell got there. If it got there from recent spills, wash the spill areas with warm water and mild soap like Woolite or Ivory liquid, then rinse and let dry. If the smell got there from years of daily swillathons, burn the rugs and sofas after removing them from the premises. Replace them with linoleum and plastic lawn furniture. If beer smell persists, offer all visitors a beer.

What's the use of getting sober when you're gonna get drunk again?

The liver is the body's only organ that can regenerate itself, stupid.

Entertaining Guys

"Creative confidence can only be permitted in neutral social territories dominated by the adolescent or by Greenwich Village. Here manners and taste have free play. But where money transactions are somehow at stake, panic enters the socially spotlighted host or hostess. It's got to be just right if it kills us."

—Marshall McLuahan, *The Mechanical Bride*

"My crib your crib."

—Ted Berrigan

Men are not natural hosts, at least in our culture. It's an acquired skill, like swimming or liking Scotch. Being a host is a lot like being a hostess, except that much less is expected of you. A woman is expected to bake a pie. A man is expected to take it out of the box and warm it up. It's not fair, but it reflects the sometimes unfortunate state of our society.

The main skill required of being a host is being able to put yourself in the guests' position. How can you make your guests happy and comfortable? For example, you might be tempted to throw a party and invite twenty girls and five guys. Unless your women friends are professional golfers they will probably not enjoy such a mix. Aim for a good balance between men and women and a good mix of personalities.

Make sure that there's something to drink for everyone. That means soft drinks, drinks without sugar, drinks with alcohol. And it may not be enough to have a case of Jagermeister or Old Milwaukee. Some people just aren't going to go for it. But once you get into being a host it can be an enormously gratifying thing. It's an artistic form of generosity. And great hosts usually have lots of fun and are often reciprocated delightfully.

I'm setting up a home bar. What kind of glasses are essential?

That all depends on your lifestyle. If you have a traditional home, you'll probably want to have a comprehensive bar with wine glasses, champagne glasses (saucers or flutes), lager glasses, high-ball glasses, rocks glasses, martini glasses, snifters, cordial glasses, and maybe port glasses. Optional glasses include sour glasses and fishbowl beer glasses. (Gonna serve ale in a lager glass, girlfriend?) If you're an oenophile (wino), you'll probably want red-wine glasses and white-wine glasses. If you have an alternative home or you're just starting out, you might just have shot glasses for shots with jelly glasses for chasers. You might want to have a small dish for Jell-O shots.

And, if you're over 40, don't forget the reading glasses.

I like to throw dinner parties for a dozen or so people. I keep it simple and it's usually fun. The problem is that I like to invite people who haven't met, but it always winds up that the old friends congregate at one end and the strangers at the other. Suggestions.

Place cards, obviously. Go for boy girl boy girl and separate spouses, steadies, and even dates. It makes it a lot more interesting, and a little competition often brings out people's most charming sides. And don't be afraid to spread the new people around the table—if you like them, chances are your friends will, too.

I'm a moderate drinker. I often entertain my friends at home. Some of them do drugs, nothing heavy but not legal either. It makes me uncomfortable. Should I say something?

Yeah. "Freeze, sucker! Take it outside." If it's happening on your property or premises, then you're bustable, too. That's an imposition. They can always take a walk around the block and not put their host in jeopardy. And if people are spending a lot of time in your bathroom, you might ask what's going on. The last thing you want to find in there is somebody with a blue complexion.

I'm having my girlfriend's parents over for dinner at my apartment. I'm nervous because I'm not much of a cook. What can I serve that will be good and within my modest capabilities?

Spaghetti or linguine with pesto sauce is pretty hard to screw up if you can boil water and follow directions. Buy a good jar of pesto sauce. Cook the pasta according to the directions on the box and don't forget to add some oil and salt to the water. The pesto doesn't need to be heated, you just add it to the pasta. Buy a piece of good Parmesan cheese and grate it yourself to be added at the table. For a salad buy some fresh arugula and dress it with extra virgin olive oil and balsamic vinegar. Add a little at a time until it's lightly coated, not soaking in it. And do this at the last minute. Some stores also sell premixed mesclun, which is a variety of tender baby greens. This is a no-effort impressive salad. Buy a nice bottle of Chianti and you have a decent meal that takes about twenty minutes to prepare and is almost foolproof.

When I have people over for dinner they usually bring something. Often it's wine. Do I have to serve the wine they brought, or can I keep it for later? Sometimes it's not too good.

You can have it whenever you like—that night, another night, never. If it's really bad, you can always take it back to their house when it's their turn. It's been common practice to serve the wines in a descending order of quality, the theory being that one's senses will be less heightened after the fourth bottle or so. Jesus was hailed for saving the best wine for last when he transformed the wine at a wedding in Cana. A pretty cool move.

I don't like people to smoke in my home. How do I tell them without being an asshole?

When they ask you for an ashtray, tell them you don't have one. Or do what New York cabbies do: put a decal on the wall that says NO SMOKING, DRIVER ALLERGIC. But if making your smoking friends seem subhuman bothers you, perhaps you should meet them in a café or park.

I'm a smoker and often wonder if I should empty all my ashtrays before guests who smoke come to visit.

Nobody likes a cigarette-butt museum. Empty all the ashtrays in your entertaining area before guests of any denomination arrive. You might also consider fluffing the pillows, washing the dishes, airing out the room, and flushing the toilet.

A friend of mine puts out his cigarettes in my house plants. He says it's good for them. Is that true?

It probably won't hurt. Farmers have been burning fields for eons to enrich the soil. But I hope your friend removes the filters after stubbing. Have you tried putting out ashtrays?

Guest Guys

"I read in a big-little nature book
that the best way to make a fire
is out of wood.
You get the wood."
—James Schuyler, from "A Picnic Cantata"

Being a good guest requires just as much panache, although not quite as much work, as being a good host. It means being thoughtful and polite and aware. It means never mooching but being a partner in the event or the household.

When you're invited for dinner at the home of friends you should contribute. Bring wine or flowers or offer to bring dessert. If your hosts have a sizable dinner and do all the work themselves, help clear the table and offer to do the dishes. Or just go in and take over. It's a great relief if a lot of prep went into the meal, and you'll definitely be high on the list for the next time.

A good overnight houseguest also pulls his weight. That means bringing wine or flowers or a gift for the house, such as scented candles or something special, maybe a tin of caviar. It also means helping out whenever possible. Make your bed in the morning. Leave the bathroom the way you found it. And don't overstay your welcome. There's an old saying that houseguests are like fish, they stink after two days.

I have a friend who likes to cook and isn't bad at it, but sometimes when I'm hanging out in the kitchen I notice he tastes the sauce (or whatever) and then puts the spoon back in the pot. This bugs me. Should I say something?

I think I have the same friend. What I did was share a theory that I'd heard once from a very good macrobiotic cook. He said one should never allow saliva to touch what you're cooking because the enzymes in it, even in very small amounts, will begin to digest the food and change its taste. I don't know if it's true, but it sounds scientific and not like you think they are unclean. Along the same lines, one of my favorite *Seinfeld* episodes is the one where George Costanza is accused by a party guest of being a "double dipper," i.e., returning a chip one has taken a bite of to the dip bowl. It's not polite and, of course, there's a long shot that it's a public health menace. I have no qualms about good-naturedly calling a foul on the double dip.

What's the deal with napkins at a dinner party? When does it go on the lap?

Etiquette says you should put it on your lap when everyone is seated. Etiquette also says that at lunch you unfold only half your napkin, but I'm ignoring that one. I'm just as messy at lunch as at dinner.

My girlfriend and I are still arguing on this one. I say "dinner at eight" means we should be there at eight. She says we should be there at eight-thirty.

William Burroughs once told me that it's rude to be on time. I show up fifteen minutes late even though my obsessive-compulsive on-time tendencies might have me walking around the block a few times. In my neck of the woods dinner at eight means that you should probably arrive between eight-fifteen and eight-thirty. This guideline does not apply to business meetings, weddings, or other ceremonial occasions when the announced time should be observed.

I recently spent a week at a friend's house in the Hamptons. My girlfriend said I should leave a tip for the maid. I said she was nuts. Who's right?

It depends. If there's a once-a-week cleaning person, no, you don't have to tip. But if there's a full-time maid who makes your bed every day and cleans and straightens up your room, you should leave a tip. For a week, twenty bucks would be appropriate.

I don't eat sugar, and I carry around packets of artificial sweetener with me. Is it rude to pull them out at someone's house?

I think in these postmodern times it's okay to bring your own poison, but before pulling it out it's probably more polite to ask for it first. There are a lot of fake sweets out there. Wouldn't you feel odd pulling out your own sugar packets at a tea party?

My circle of friends gives dinner parties fairly often, sometimes with assigned seats. My girlfriend always wants to sit next to me, although sometimes the host or hostess deliberately separates couples. Recently I caught her moving a place card. How bad is that?

Pretty bad. It indicates that she is insanely jealous, cripplingly shy, or plain rude. Or all of the above. The whole point of making a seating plan for a party is to introduce people or mix things up in an amusing way. Is your girlfriend possessive in other ways? Is she shy? If you let her get away with subverting your hosts' plan, you are guilty by association. Get to the bottom of it. I'm sure you're fond of the lass, but this rearranging streak of hers could indicate codependence, antisocial tendencies, and the control-freak syndrome. Don't marry her until you've worked this problem out.

A friend of mine—not a very close one—is getting married soon, and I'm invited to attend with a date. My new girlfriend used to date the best man. Should I bring her or invite a friend?

Who's uncomfortable, you or her? Do I sense a little jealousy? I think you should invite her and let her decide if she wants to go. If she doesn't, maybe you should just go solo.

I have a wedding coming up soon, and I don't have a gift yet. A friend told me that you have a year to come up with a gift. Is this true? Should I send a "gift IOU"?

No need. And, yes, you do have a year. But as the months go by, it gets easier to forget about it.

A very good friend of mine is getting married. Love him, hate her. Does the gift have to be for both of them?

What were you thinking of? A bowling ball? Boxer shorts? Towels that say "His"? Of course the gift has to be for both of them.

My best pal is renewing his wedding vows. (It was her idea.) Do I have to throw him another bachelor party?

Do you mean as a last chance to violate his old vows? No, I don't think so. Maybe a poker party or a golf outing but forget the strippers, etc. The guy is married.

When I visited my last girlfriend at her parents' house, I put my bags in her room and everyone got upset. I have a new girlfriend and the same situation is coming up. How do I handle it?

Let her handle it. It doesn't really matter what room you're in, although you don't want to be on a Castro convertible in the living room. Chances are that her parents will have given the arrangements as much thought as you have. It's their call.

I'm totally intimidated at dinner parties. I don't know what fork to use when. I don't know what glass to use when. Help!

Usually the silver is set down in the order you're supposed to use it in. From left to right. If there's a salad first, you'll usually find a salad fork on the extreme left of your fork array. If you have any doubt, the salad fork is usually smaller. But if you're totally stumped, just keep an eye on the host or a confident guest and follow their lead.

What are you supposed to do with all those fancy hand towels people leave in the bathroom at a party?

If they're hanging on the rack, replace them neatly. If there's a big stack of them, there should be a basket to toss them in when you're finished. If there is no basket, throw it on the floor, go to your host, exclaim "Someone has taken the hand towel basket!" and laugh strangely.

I've been vegetarian for three years now. I'm not morally opposed to killing animals, I just don't like meat. I hate having to explain my preferences. Is there a tactful way to let others know this without sounding offensive or ungrateful when invited to dine?

If you're eating at someone's home, the best thing, my macrobiotic pals advise, is to eat what you can and leave the rest. (Not on your plate, in the serving dish.) You don't have to explain why you don't eat any particular item. In fact it's much better not to reveal your dietary philosophy when you're a dinner guest. You can always explain your diet, if anyone is interested, on another occasion. I am morally opposed to killing animals, but I eat meat on moral grounds because if we all stopped eating meat, then pigs and chickens would be unemployed and soon thereafter extinct.

Traveling Guys

"I chanced to be in Miles' white Ferrari when he was driving it up the West Side Highway at about 105 miles per hour. Frances got very frightened and asked him to slow down. Miles gave her the perfect Milesian reply. 'I'm in here too.'"

—Joe Goldberg, quoted in *Milestones,*
the *Music and Times of Miles Davis* by Jack Chambers

"For my part, I travel not to go anywhere, but to go. I travel for travel's sake. The great affair is to move."

—Old Bob Lou Stevenson

Traveling broadens your mind, and it can broaden your perspective, your circle of friends, your wardrobe. It's the least harmful and most enjoyable way to alter your consciousness. And it's fun.

How much do you tip a bellman in a hotel? I always feel like I'm tipping too little or too much.

A dollar a bag is appropriate on check-in and checkout. The same you would tip a baggage handler at an airport. (A very important place to tip if you want your baggage to end up at the same airport you do.) If the bellman renders you some special service like carrying something heavy or finding you a date, then he should be compensated additionally. And don't forget to leave a little something for the maid. It's not easy being a maid.

I always wind up sitting next to people's kids on airplanes. Often the parents are sitting elsewhere. I'm not a kid hater, but I like to sleep on planes and they often make it hard.

Try faking a bad cough. Or carrying a copy of Hustler or Barely Legal might get their parents' attention. Then offer to switch seats with the parents.

I always get lousy hotel rooms. Is it something I'm wearing? How can I get better rooms?

Ask for one. Just say that you don't like it, it's not acceptable, what else do they have? You'd be surprised how many people do this, and it usually works. The hotels often try to fill the worst rooms first because they're expecting that the person that comes in after you will be pickier.

I'm the worst at packing. When I unpack, everything looks like I've slept in it. Any ideas on how I can transport my stuff so it looks good when I arrive?

This is my weak spot, I confess. I always try to get female help. They just seem to know what they're doing. Having the right luggage helps. Even though I'm deeply committed to carry-on, having spent a few years of my life waiting at luggage carousels, I like to try to take a hanging bag, so my suits and even my shirts can stay on hangers. Another key principle is not packing too much. Cram that stuff in there and you might as well just use a laundry bag as luggage. Pack clothes that wear well. A linen suit is going to look wrinkled after five minutes of wearing, so maybe it's not the best choice for traveling. Let's see—um, no hardcover books, that's now a rule for me. Stuff your shoes with socks and don't take too many pairs of socks. They are sink-washable. Get travel-size toiletries—a little can of shaving cream, a small tube of toothpaste, a folding travel toothbrush. Always take a bathing suit. You never know.

And don't forget to get some little padlocks to lock your luggage. It's a mean world. And don't forget the keys. And don't forget to put your name on your luggage. Maybe you'll see it again.

When I fly I go for sweatpants and a sweatshirt. Am I gross?

Not necessarily. We sometimes long for the days of the well-dressed sophisticated traveler, but we're not going first class on the *Titanic* here. I think you can take a tip from Virgin Atlantic's "Upper Class" where they issue what is basically a sweat suit for overnight Transatlantic passengers to change into. If you're going to sleep, you might as well get as close to jammies as you can.

I'm making my first trip to Europe. How do I avoid looking like an Ugly American?

I'm guessing that you already know. Don't wear hockey jerseys, baseball caps, or advertising T-shirts. There are plenty of badly dressed people in Europe, but Americans still have a knack for standing out. Just observe the rules of good taste. Don't under-dress. Try to look like a gentleman. You know how to do it. If you don't, rent a movie with gentlemen in it and observe.

How do you deal with jet lag?

Try not to get it. When heading to Europe from America, see if you can't find a day flight. There's still one to London. I've been called an old man and unbusinesslike for taking the day flight (not to mention refusing the L.A.-to-N.Y. red-eye), but look who's alert at midnight and nine in the morning. If you must fly to Europe at night, go to sleep immediately. Before they serve cocktails and dinner. Before the movie. You might take a melatonin a half hour before you want to hit dreamland. (It will help you sleep, and some say it will re-adjust your body clock. Take one milligram; don't take the three-milligram unless you like grogginess.) If you're not an addictive type, you might use a prescription your doctor has provided. (Some people swear by the no-hangover Ambien. But gimme a Valium and a double espresso in the morning.) On the way back just stay up until your usual bedtime. What jet lag?

What is it with the regulations on using laptops, cellular phones, and electronic games on an airplane? Do these really pose any threat to the plane?

It is conceivable that some electronic equipment could interfere with one of a plane's many electronic systems. I have flown on private jets though, and we're cell-phoning all the way, so I suspect it's really about this: Do you want three hundred yakkers with their cell phones ringing away madly on a densely packed can of humans? The best thing to do is follow the rules, which usually means you're free to use your laptop between takeoff and landing modes. Just make sure that it doesn't intrude on your neighbors' turf.

My dad once told me the best way to travel in a car with a jacket is to hold it at the back of the neck and fold it in half inside out and lay it down.

Yes, that is probably the best way, short of hanging it on a hanger and hanging the hanger on the hanger doohickey in the backseat. Obviously this won't work in many cars, including the Porsche Boxster, so your dad was right. I myself like to use the traditional hanger method, mainly because it gives my dog something to shed on in the backseat.

How do you get upgraded on planes?

Get a gold or platinum frequent-flier card. Use a platinum card to pay for your ticket and beg for an upgrade. Tell them you're a travel writer. Be nice, don't threaten or be demanding. Have a bad back. Dress nicely. Tell them your next leg is twenty hours. Don't be afraid to plead. If it doesn't work, ask for the bulkhead or exit row.

Guys on the Town

"Ou est le N.Y. Times?"

—Robert Benchley

Style is the way you live your life. It's especially evident when you're living it up, living large. Someone can fake looking like a gentlemen, but you can't fake acting like one. The way you carry yourself, they way you interact with others, that's the true test of a person with great style.

Does slipping a maître d' a tip like they do in the movies get you a better table? If so, how much do you slip?

The Magic 8 Ball says, "Don't count on it."

Is it pretentious to use French phrases when you're speaking in English?

Bien sûr! Although *comme ci, comme ça* is *comme ci, comme ça*.

I love music and enjoy the atmosphere of clubs, but I'm really uncomfortable dancing, even after a few drinks. How can I learn to dance? I don't need to waltz, just basic boogie.

You probably know how. You just need the will to boogie. I'd suggest boogying solo at home at every opportunity. There's always dancing school, but maybe you should sign up for an aerobic course at your local gym. Maybe if you get those muscles used to moving, it will just come to you.

When I go on a date I never know what to order. If I order what I like, it's usually messy or full of garlic or gives me gas. Can you recommend a menu strategy?

Messy food isn't a great idea for a first-date dinner. Forget whole lobsters or spaghetti with red sauce. Ixnay on the meatball sandwich or the overstuffed hot pastrami. You should be able to handle most normal entrées without too much problem. Just eat slowly and avoid things that you have to crack open or tend to slurp. As for garlic, it's not a problem if you both eat it, and it could give you some conversational fodder. As for gas, it's true what they say about beans. Save them till you're engaged.

I pretty much follow the 15 percent to 20 percent rule for most restaurant meals. My question is about minimum and maximum tips. I generally tip a dollar a head no matter how small the bill. I have a problem with what to tip on the high end. If I'm out with friends at a nice place and we have a few bottles of wine, the bill can hit $500. Is it really customary to tip $75 to $100 on a bill this size?

If the bill is high because of the wine, you can tip 15 percent instead of 20 percent. If the bill is high because you have a larger group, and you've had excellent service, then 20 percent would still be in order. Many restaurants automatically add a 15 percent to 20 percent tip for groups of eight or more. Make sure a tip hasn't been added before paying the bill. If a restaurant has a wine steward, you may tip him or her 10 percent of the wine charge and tip the waiter the usual amount on the food and cocktails.

How much should you tip a washroom attendant?

I will go out of my way to find an unattended washroom, but sometimes they've got you and you've got to use it. As soon as you leave the stall or urinal, they've got the tap on and the towel out. You can make a run for the door, if you're confident about your hand hygiene. But basically you're trapped by this guy who spends forty hours a week in a toilet. It's worse than squeegee guys on the street. If you tip more than a dollar, you're encouraging them to occupy even more men's rooms. If you leave less, they may give you the evil eye. Take a mint and give 'em a buck. But not a crisp one. Maybe one that you peed on.

Why do waiters ask if I want my salad after my main course?

They think you come from Europe where salad often comes after. That could be taken as a compliment. Maybe it's the way you hold your knife and fork. Lots of people like salad afterward because they believe it's better in the digestive scheme of things. Don't worry, pumpkin, you can have your salad anytime you want no matter where you are.

The past few times I've been at buffet breakfasts or brunches my friends and I have argued about tipping. They say that you don't tip at all because you're getting your own food. I believe you should tip at least a small portion, as the waiter is bringing you some things. Am I nuts, or are they cheap?

Cheap. Chances are the wait staff is still making a minimum wage on buffet days. What's a minimal 10 percent when it's all-you-can-eat, huh? Actually waiters have told me that working a buffet is just as taxing as regular service, so 15 percent won't kill you.

Physical Guys

"I remember the skinny guy who gets sand kicked in his face in body-building advertisements."

—Joe Brainard, *I Remember*

Nobody's perfect. Everybody has something about their physical being that they would like to change. Sometimes you can change it and sometimes you can't. There's an AA slogan that's a good approach to one's physical being. "God, grant me the serenity to accept the things I cannot change, the courage to change the things I can, and the wisdom to know the difference."

I'm a tall, thin guy (6'3", 190 pounds). What type of clothes should I avoid?

Tight clothes. Remember the *Seinfeld* episode where Kramer puts on the skintight jeans. Actually the regular Kramer look, with a few modifications, is a good look for tall, thin guys. Think relaxed and comfortable. Anything too tight will just make you look geeky. Howard Stern has many fine attributes, but the guy's clothes are too narrow.

I've had my left ear pierced for seven years and was pondering piercing my right ear, as well. Is it fashionable for a man to have both of his ears pierced?

This is just one of those taste matters. To me, dual pierced ears look fairly stupid on guys unless they are wearing really big drop earrings and need to balance their head. Of course, just because both ears are pierced doesn't mean that you have to wear two earrings at all times. You could alternate. Left ear one day, right ear the next. You could pick which ear according to your mood. The left ear could wear the ring on days where you feel left-brained and vice versa. Or one side could signal dominant days, the other submissive days.

I wore an earring throughout my college years. I've been in the corporate world for six years and haven't worn it since; however, the hole is still there. Is there any way to fix the hole? I suspect it's not helping my career.

Wow, you must have been wearing a real Carmen Miranda dangler. Most post holes fill up all by themselves. A plastic surgeon can make your earlobe look pristine for a couple of hundred bucks, give or take.

There is a small mole on my face that I don't like. How do you get rid of it?

You don't. Maybe a doctor can, but maybe he'll tell you to learn to like it. Why don't you do what corporations do and have a focus group. Ask your friends if they like it. If they do, maybe you can learn to, too.

I joined a gym and lost fifteen pounds. Is it worth getting all my suits altered? If I put the weight back, can they alter them back?

Was it Columbus who burned the ships so the crew had to stick it out in the New World? Yeah, alter those suits. Welcome to the New World, Slim. But if you have a lot of suits, you might want to leave a few fat suits just in case. Can you alter them back? Sure. You might want to confide your fears to your tailor, just to be sure.

I have these horrible bags under my eyes. It spoils my face! What can I do?

According to my macrobiotic friends, maybe you should have your kidneys checked. You might try getting more sleep and cut down on the booze. Or, if it's more of a genetic design flaw than a lifestyle problem, and you're not ready for surgery, there are a few options. Ice works. They say Paul Newman soaks his face in ice water before going on camera. Ice definitely tightens up the loose ends. You can get a gel-filled eye mask that you keep in the freezer and put it on for a quick fix. Or there's the old cucumber-slices-on-the-lids technique. It won't eliminate bags completely. And of course, there's the old Las Vegas face-lift, which involves applying Preparation H, which contains a powerful astringent, to sagging areas of the face. But I warn you, don't try this without speaking to your doctor first. Eyes are sensitive. And you might feel like an asshole.

Is plastic surgery okay for guys?

Is plastic surgery okay for anyone, is more the question. Sometimes plastic surgery is a good thing. If you have a horrible schnozzola that makes you miserable, it's okay to have it honed down to a nose you can love. Just tell any potential mother of your children that the nose in your genes is not the one on your face. As far as plastic surgery for aging goes, does a guy really want to wind up shaving behind his ears? I'm of the opinion that aging can make you look even handsomer. Look at Henry Fonda or Jimmy Stewart. This is one area where men have it all over women. You can be a sex symbol practically till you drop.

The last couple of months I've lost a relatively large amount of weight. This is good, but the excess skin around my midsection is not. Is there anything short of surgery to get rid of the unwanted skin?

Chances are you'll tighten up some eventually, but why not replace that vanished flab with some muscle and fill out some skin. Toning the muscles will help tighten up your skin.

I'm an aspiring model with a big nose. Do you have any advice?

Don't despair until you've been turned away by everyone. Sometimes a big nose is just a great nose. Johnny Zander, who's very successful, has a sizable schnozzola. So does the actor Richard Edson. Not to mention the great Bob Hope. Remember, they all told Lauren Hutton to get the gap in her teeth fixed, and it became her trademark. If you're still worried, rent *Cyrano de Bergerac* starring Gérard Depardieu, and it might help you love the thing.

Do you have any advice about staying fit? How do you stay in shape?

My advice is don't get a whole lot of muscles you don't need. They spoil the line of your clothes. Style Guy believes in the bike, the treadmill, and walking the golf course whenever possible. Of course, certain body parts are going to probably need remedial work. I do stomach stuff, which also helps the back. But be careful. Do your sit-ups and abs stuff right and avoid the hernia above the navel that kept Style Guy off the links for months.

I have a fat face, and I was wondering how I could make my face a little skinnier.

Stop eating so much maybe? But if you're not fat elsewhere, you could just be the baby-fat type. The good news is it will probably go away. The bad news is it might take a few years. If you have a wide face, you could try a different hairstyle and/or facial hair to give you some verticality. Maybe a Kramer hi-rise on top and a Fu Manchu on the chin.

All you ever hear about these days is losing weight, but I'm practically a walking stick. I've tried liquid weight gainers, but they always fill me up so I can't eat anything else. Do you have any ideas?

Short of seeing a nutritionist . . . Guinness Stout? Beer seems to be the most fattening thing I've discovered. I'm terrified of it. You might also try violating all the current diets by combining plenty of proteins and carbos. Meat and potatoes. Burger and fries. Like that.

I work out regularly, I watch what I eat, and I still have love handles. Should I be thinking about liposuction?

Whaddya, nuts? Liposuction should be considered only by those being moved around in wheelbarrows, those who lose sandwiches in the folds. Otherwise diet and exercise should be enough to make you healthy and presentable, if not godlike. If you're really eating right and exercising enough and you still have love handles, learn to love them, and others will, too.

Is cosmetic dentistry okay for men?

Did you think it was just for women? I'm forgetting that you asked.

I'm getting married in a few months. How can I make sure the occasional pimple is a no-show at the wedding?

Lay off the candy bars till your honeymoon. You can also use a good mask occasionally to keep your pores open. I like Kiehl's clay mask (available at the best department stores). Any good astringent mask will help. Spread it on, let it harden, and wash it off. It feels great and keeps your skin supermodel fresh. You can also use a cleanser designed for oily skin. There are lots of them. Ask your fiancée or check the beauty counter at a better drugstore.

If, however, despite all your precautions, a hideous zit should manifest itself before an important and photogenic occasion, there are remedies. You can cover it up, sort of. This is one of the few nondrag occasions for men in makeup. I'm not suggesting you wear foundation, like a TV weatherman or a politician on a chat show. But a little bit of foundation (ask the bride, ask the bridesmaids, ask your girlfriend or your mother) applied directly on the blemish can sometimes make it seem to disappear. If you're living in an urban center or have very stylish female contacts, you might even gain access to an undereye cover stick or concealer, an important weapon in the arsenal of many makeup-wise vixens. This cosmetic item was created to make things disappear. Why should women have all the tricks? A good one is Philosophy's Trust Me. They have an 800 number. I'm looking for it on all these Post-its. Call 800 information, okay? I'm busy.

But here's a secret for when you've got a hideous pimple that hasn't popped. Fluoride toothpaste. Crest, for example. Apply to the pimple and you might nip it in the bud. Honest.

Every summer my thighs break out with unsightly red bumps. I've tried baby powder, corn starch, and all-cotton underwear. I still get them. What could be causing them?

It sounds like ingrown hairs. Are you wearing something tighter in the hot season? You might try wearing softer, looser underwear to minimize chafing. The Gap makes some nice knit cotton boxers that aren't pricey. If loosening up doesn't work, you might try an over-the-counter cortisone cream like Cortaid. If that doesn't work, go see a doctor. It could be heat rash. Or you might have pityriasis rosea or folliculitis, neither of which is fatal. Either way, doc can probably help with some soothing, healing preparation.

My teeth are a sort of butter yellow. I smoke. I don't brush after every meal. Is there any hope?

Yeah, the dentist can bleach your teeth. Or you can do it yourself. Check out a Rembrandt Dazzling White kit and follow the directions. If you can stand not rinsing for twenty minutes, you can have white teeth.

I have a good build, but my rear end is as flat as a pancake. A girl at work teases me about this constantly. Any suggestions?

I never realized how much women are into guys' butts. They like butt as much as we do. And today it's painfully obvious that a good set of male buns has the power to mesmerize many vixens.

Go to your local video store and rent or buy *Buns of Steel: Beginners*. I tested this video myself and found that my butt tightened considerably. I also loved being ordered around by fitness expert Tamilee Webb, M.A., who is, herself, a constant reminder of the primal allure of tighter, steelier buns. Hers are among the curviest and most flabless buns I have observed. And, under the tutelage of this tush expert, I did change my derriere for the better, although I never wanted to go for total buffness back there, since I'm kind of against excess muscle anywhere. I like a body that looks good in a suit. I now have adequate *tokhes*, as they say in Yiddish, and my guess is that with two months of religious *Buns of Steel* work, your duff will be plenty buff. I think it's just what the buttophile ordered.

How do you tell your date that they have spinach in their teeth?

"You look beautiful, even with spinach in your teeth."

I'm 5′6″ and 135 pounds. I like classics like Tommy Hilfiger and Polo/Ralph Lauren. The fact is that the clothes in the boys' department fit me better and are significantly less expensive. When I shop in the boys' department I get strange looks from the salesladies.

Let 'em look. The big sizes in the boys' department are as big as or bigger than the smallest sizes in men's. (In most cases a 20 equals a 34.) The only real difference is the price. I know plenty of men who shop in boys—hey, there are some big boys out there. I even know women who buy boys' suits and have them cut down, because boys' are much cheaper than women's suits, often with a higher level of workmanship. If the salesladies give you a hard time, tell them you're a jockey and give them a bum tip on the horses.

It seems like no matter how much I weigh, I always have pointy breasts. Guys rag on me in the locker room. Is there an exercise I can do to shape up my pecs and not be pointy?

Some men have gynecomastia, which doctors can help with. It's more about hormones than muscle tone. And it doesn't mean that you're a girl trapped in a man's body or vice versa. But you might try working out with a trainer and have them walk you through the upper-body machines. If you work the upper body enough, you might still point, but who's going to rag on you in the locker room?

Guys' Stuff

"In the world of Advertisement ... everything that happens today ... is better, bigger, brighter, more astonishing than anything that has ever existed before.... The essence of this living-in-the-moment and for-the-moment is ... to banish all individual continuity.... Your personality must have been chopped down to an extremely low level of purely reactionary life. Otherwise you are of no use to the advertiser."

—Wyndham Lewis, *Time and Western Man*

Guys are collectors. Guys are hoarders. They are hobbyists, fanatics, and freaks. They define themselves by their stuff. But men are specialists. They'll know everything about Studebakers or stereos or Eskimo masks or Louisville Sluggers or microbrews and nothing about the sheets they're sleeping on or the towels they're wrapped in.

But our stuff is often the way that our spirits make contact with the material world. We live in a fetish culture. Our stuff is our arsenal, our bag of tricks, our lore, our sacred artifacts. We love our tools, our golf clubs, our fountain pens and overpriced watches. We can't help it. But it's okay. We should love our stuff. But only if we love one another first.

I own a 1982 Oldsmobile Cutlass in good shape. I'd like to make it more stylish without making it look tacky. What accessories would go well, aside from tinted windows? Please don't say fuzzy dice.

I don't like dice, and besides, hanging things from the rearview is illegal in many states. I've got to say that I'm a purist in this area.

There are exceptions, but generally nothing is cooler than a stock automobile. The best improvements are invisible, like upgraded brakes and shocks, or a six CD changer in the trunk. Even adding a tach is kind of tacky.

How do I smoke a cigar without looking like a pretentious prick?

Undo your little ponytail, turn the collar of your polo shirt down, put away the cellular phone, cut back on the tanning gel, and don't drive a car with a spoiler. Oh, and take the band off before you smoke the cigar. Unless, of course, you're wearing a Davidoff T-shirt or baseball cap. See below.

My friend says you leave bands on cigars, I say you take them off before smoking. Who's right?

There are two schools on this one. Being discreet to the point of affectation (I took the chrome model number off the back of my car), I remove the bands before smoking. I've noticed that most smokers do not, apparently on the theory "If you've got it, flaunt it." But one friend of mine says it's okay to leave them on, lest you damage the wrapper in removing the band. So if someone calls you on egregious Cubano Cohiba flaunting, at least you've got an excuse. By the way, you can always save your old bands and donate them to the divorce lawyer, spec home builder, or used Porsche dealer of your choice.

My lover wants to buy me a bracelet. What kind looks cool on a guy?

ID bracelets can have a certain Rat Pack cachet. Heavy drinkers can engrave them with their name and last known address. Bad drivers can engrave them with their blood type. Let's see, what else is there? Medic Alert bracelets aren't really cool unless you need one. Those copper antiarthritis bracelets don't look bad. Maybe I'm old-fashioned, but I think the best-looking bracelet for men has a sports watch attached.

Am I being judged by my pen?

Yes and no. It's more important what comes out of it, but pens are sometimes mightier than the sword or PC. Being frequently paid by the word, I love my PowerBook, my PowerPC, my Sharpies, my Bulgari ballpoint (an expensive gift, but a triumph of design and the perfect weight for inking powerful metaphors), and my Mont Blanc fountain pen and roller ball. Also it would be hard to live without a Pilot Precise Rolling Ball V5 Extra Fine, some Eberhard Faber Uni-Balls, and a box of disposable Pilot fountain pens. Nothing signs a letter, a thank-you note, a passionate missive, or an affidavit better than a fountain pen. That signature just flows. And, next to old watches and vintage cars, few things are as fun to collect as old pens.

I realize the urban thump machine may offend fellow motorists. What type of car audio components do you recommend?

I think it's not so much the components, as how they are used. I don't think that any car really needs mega bass, except, of course, those U.S. Army Humvees that surrounded General Noriega of Panama's palace and forced him to surrender by playing Jimi Hendrix day and night. But high-powered stereos are okay as long as you don't turn the volume knob too far clockwise. Waking innocent sleepers is criminal. I simply keep the windows up while blasting the Miles Davis Quintet. My ride has fifteen speakers and hundreds of watts, and I have never turned it to the max except just this once when, driven mad by the criminal loudspeakers of the neighboring Hampton Classic Horse Show, I did a drive-by while playing NWA's "Fuck tha Police" at full volume. It gave me a great deal of satisfaction.

I just rented a new apartment. I love the neighborhood and building, but the space itself is really generic, unlike my bohemian lifestyle and flea market furniture. How can I spice up the typical white-box apartment?

Paint it. That's a good first step. Something that keeps the place light but kills any resemblance to a bad art gallery. Flea market furniture can be great, especially if it's mixed in with some modern pieces. If you're bohemian, then go eclectic, baby. And you might want to put something on those walls. If you can't afford paintings, you can start with old movie posters or travel posters, which can be found at antique shows and won't cost you an arm and a leg. Good photographs can also be affordable. The thing is to go with what you like, not what somebody says you should like. Decorating your pad, like dressing yourself, is a way to complement your personality. Let it hang out.

I just redid my bathroom. It's all white. I need new towels. My significant other suggested ditching white or light blue for something with a pattern. My tastes are generally more conservative than hers. Also I hate lint. What do you suggest?

My answer depends on whose bathroom it is. If it's yours, go with your own taste and get white. If you share the premises, you may have to flip for it or go to a linen counselor. I myself have nothing but white towels. Maybe it's a fetish, but that way I know they're really clean. As for lint, any good brand such as Fieldcrest or Ralph Lauren should be lint-free after the first washing. See your local upscale department store or try a good catalog like Chambers or The Company Store. These catalogs often carry the top brands of towels made for hotels. These are very well made, launder well, and last a long time.

I'm in the watch market. Should I get one expensive watch or several less expensive ones to go with different things?

I think it's good to have several. If you have only one, a classic sports watch, like a steel Rolex, TAG Heuer, etc., is acceptable for dressy occasions but will also have what it takes to survive vigorous sports activities, swimming, and bar fighting. Steel is much more affordable than gold and more fashion acceptable than black. Style Guy loves the classical Swatches—last purchase: Gary Panter's homage to Brooklyn. They're excellently water resistant and may even appreciate in value. My old Keith Harings are worth a mod fortune today. Once you've got a good all-purpose watch, you can add a dressy watch when you can afford it.

I would like to invest in a watch this year, and I'm willing to spend up to $2500. How can I tell what is a great product and what is crap with a designer name?

Forget designer watches and go with a watch that's from a great watchmaking company like Rolex (including the lower-priced Tudor line), Movado, TAG Heuer, Vacheron, Breitling, Cartier, Tiffany, Audemars Piguet. Swiss watches have deserved their reputation for elegance but there are other fine watches. Style Guy owns and loves an old Hamilton (which was the watch of American railroad conductors during the great days of railroads) and a Bulova Accutron (the original quartz watch) as well as some oldie Audemars Piguet models. You can find great vintage watches that are good as new.

I'm a Wall Street investment banker in my late twenties. This year, thanks to the boom, I got a six-figure bonus. I live well, but I haven't made any major purchases except a Porsche and a serious stereo. I like good furniture and art, but I want to invest wisely. Where do I start?

Research. Get out there and see what appeals to you. Your taste is in there somewhere trying to get out. Once you buy that first piece of good furniture or art, it gives you a direction, and things sort of fall into place. You could hire a designer, but if you take it slow, it's more fun to do it yourself. Check out the antique stores, including those with classic modern furniture. Visit the galleries. Pick up art magazines like *ArtForum* or *Art in America*. This is a lot better time to buy art than during the last stock boom of the eighties. Consult the experts, then consult your heart. The best investments in furniture and art are the things that will appreciate in value but that you'll never want to part with.

My wallet is too fat. Not that I'm rich, but with several credit cards, money, and all, it seems very bulky in my back pocket. What's the answer?

I don't believe in carrying money in your wallet. If your wallet is too fat, it will create a bulge in your pants, and not an attractive bulge. It might even throw off your sitting posture and lead to lower back pain. It's easier to keep bills in a money clip in a side pocket. (Tiffany makes a great silver money clip that is in fact a large silver paper clip.) Here's what you need in your wallet: Driver's license and registration, a couple of credit cards, bank card, HMO card, a couple of business cards, and maybe a few checks. Even if you're a credit card collector, do you need to carry them all at all times? Rotate those Visas and MasterCards like crops. Women have the luxury of carrying around photos of all of their friends, relatives, and pets because they carry purses. If you're going to sit on that wallet, keep it slim.

I have a lot of sweaters that have developed pills that ruin their looks. What can I do about them?

Pilling happens to sweaters. It's more likely to happen to cheaper sweaters, but it can happen to better sweaters, too. One way to help prevent pilling is to turn your sweaters inside out when you wash them. Pills can be removed by shaving them off. There are small electric shavers made especially for this purpose, or you can shave them off with a regular razor. Just take it slow and easy and stay on the surface. There's no quick way to do it.

Is there a way to remove or clean the sweat smell out of a leather watchband? I've tried using mild soap and water, which does not seem to do the trick.

Does it really smell that much? Do people back off when you enter the room? If saddle soap doesn't work, maybe you need to consult a doctor. Or buy a new watchband. Have you ever noticed that sports watches come with metal bracelets? Maybe they're trying to tell you something.

My girlfriend recently found lipstick on my collar. How can I get lipstick off immediately?

You're planning on doing it again? Lipstick comes off in the wash, so all you have to do is beat the poor woman you are betraying to the washing machine and use a little Spray 'n Wash on the spot before washing it. You can also rub a little spot remover (like DiDi Seven, found at better hardware stores) on the lipstick and rinse until the stain is gone. The stain on your character may prove more difficult to remove.

What can I do with my white dress shirts so they're less wrinkled at the end of the day?

If you send your shirts out, ask the cleaners to do them with light starch and on a hanger, not folded. If you do them yourself, use a small amount of spray starch. Or you can also use sizing. This is the stuff that keeps your shirt so crisp when it comes from the store. It also comes in a spray can.

I picked up a sharp black suit at a vintage store, but it has this musty, old-guy smell. I've had it cleaned three times, but it still has unwanted aroma. Ideas?

Hang it outside on a line to air out. Don't put it in the direct sun though, or you'll have a sort-of-gray, sort-of-black suit. You also might throw a little cologne in the lining, too.

A blue Bic exploded in the pocket of my chinos. What can I do about it?

Style Guy once had a Mont Blanc fountain pen leak in the pocket of a favorite shirt. Now he wears the shirt under a sweater or when turning the compost heap. But a styley colleague reports that Aqua Net, an aerosol hairspray, can be used to dissolve ink. He says you soak tissues with the hairspray and blot, don't rub, from both sides. Then wash as usual. Style Guy has tried DiDi Seven, the megastrength stain remover, but maybe he was a little late. Let me know. I have an Eberhard Faber Uni-Ball that looks like it's ready to blow.

Guys with Hobbies

"Gifted athletes venture onto the terrain of the artist almost as often as the reverse is the case.... In 1977 the multitalented Billy Martin exhibited at the posh Pace Gallery on Manhattan's Fifty-seventh Street, a startling series of junked refrigerator doors smashed into likenesses of his patron, George Steinbrenner. The critics gave Martin high marks for surface tension, structural integrity, originality in choice of materials, and the use of the sledge, but most of all for passion, without which neither art nor baseball would signify at all."

—Donald Barthelme, *The Art of Baseball*

know a lot of people who go to shrinks, and I think that a lot of them would do better with a really good hobby. I don't mean drinking or drugs, I mean something that can really occupy your mind and be productive or educational or even profitable. Collecting is good. Long after the stock market crashes, my book collection will be worth something.

I like to take pictures. I'm not a pro, but I'm getting pretty good. The problem is that I live in a small town and I'd like to get better processing and prints than are available through the local drug-store. Any ideas?

There are quite a few good film labs that you can deal with by mail. Try the Seattle Film Works, P.O. Box 34056, Seattle, WA 98124-1056. Web site: www.filmworks.com. E-mail: info@filmworks.com. Phone: 800-FILMWORKS.

What is it with golf clothes? Why do golfers dress that way?

Well, the pros get paid to dress that way. I'm never going to wear a visor that says "Buick" on the course, but if they offered me six figures, I might consider it. As a proud amateur I'm of the opinion that the best golf clothes are regular clothes. It's part of the great charm of the sport. I love to see pictures of the old masters playing in long white shirts and ties. That's the genius of golf. You can play it in the same clothes that you wear for the rest of your life. And maybe, if you can't take a full athletic swing, your suit is too tight. The old guys wore ties, and they hit it a ton. Marketers will try to convince you that there is such a thing as golf clothes. There is no such thing. Knit shirts are obviously a good choice, but a well-cut dress shirt shouldn't restrict your swing.

Somebody once said that golf was a sport that enabled white guys to dress like blacks. And it's true that some men need an excuse to wear bright green trousers. But I figure, God bless. The Republicans came up with the trickle-down theory. Maybe there's a fashion equivalent.

I love music. I have a great stereo. My downstairs neighbor is always harassing me for playing my music too loud. How late can I play it without being guilty?

It's hard to say what hours are okay. We don't all live by the same clock. But maybe you can do something about it. It's amazing what carpeting can do to dampen the sound issuing from an apartment. Try carpeting. Try not mounting your speakers on the walls. Try dialogue. It can't hurt. Or try headphones.

Should I get a DVD?

You don't have one yet? Run, boy. It's the best thing for movies; you can store what would be a cartonload of tape in a little booklet. You can listen to music on it. You can access randomly instead of, yawn, rewinding. It's the future; it's not another Betamax.

Nutty Guys

"… one of the consequences of Dandyism … its most general characteristic—is its ability always to produce the unexpected, something for which a mind accustomed to the yoke of routine cannot in sound logic be prepared."

—**Barbey D'Aurevilley, *The Anatomy of Dandyism* with some observations of Beau Brummell**

You think this is easy? You try giving advice. Everything here was learned the hard way, by trial and error, by error and error, by embarrassment, mortification, and the irrepressible life force and the creative imperative. If you don't like it, that's too bad. I gave it my best shot.

Sometimes Style Guy gets questions that make him suspect the sincerity and/or sanity of the querant. A few of these are reproduced here.

One morning I woke up to find the dead body of a fifty-year-old hooker in my bed. There was drug paraphernalia all over my bedroom dresser, and the walls were speckled with blood and vomit. The Beatles' White Album was playing backwards. Should I use a sponge or an old wet T-shirt to clean up?

First try playing the White Album forward and it may just clean itself up. Otherwise call the police and let them clean up.

I have a male friend who would like to know of a company that makes good cosmetics for men. He's most interested in foundations.

You forgot to mention whether he was a politician, an anchorman, or a drag queen with a heavy beard. Actually, hon, guys and gals use the same kinds of foundation. Certain products are skewed toward a gender because sometimes it makes you feel more like a man if you're wearing a men's deodorant, but really it's all marketing. And most of the men who are foundation customers probably like wearing a women's brand, eh?

Glenn, man, you gotta help me out. You're my last hope. When I was a young boy my mother told me not to touch the baby birds in the nest in the maple tree in my front yard. She said that the mother robin would abandon her young and leave them to fend for themselves. Is this just one of those hoaxes like the Santa Claus bit or the real thing?

It's true. Don't do it again.

How do you make your penis bigger? Do I have to eat anything to make it bigger?

Try thinking happy thoughts. If that doesn't work, try eating footlong hot dogs, cucumbers, zucchini, carrots, parsnips, bananas, etc. If that doesn't help, try putting them in your pants.

Do animals have souls?

Yes, especially dogs. Cats have souls but they are wanton killers. If you suddenly became six inches tall, your cats would kill you, after an amusing torture interlude. Your dog, however, would still sit on command. Rats have the reincarnated souls of dead divorce lawyers.

How common is it for people to be in therapy? How can you tell if you need to go?

It is very common to be in therapy. It's good to be getting better. Usually the best way to tell if you need to go is when your friends ask if you've considered it. Hint, hint.

Epilogue

"The technology now exists to change dramatically everyone's way of looking at the world, past, present and future. One has only to think of Gorbachev's first four years in power. Seventy years of demonizing the Soviet Union was expertly undone by his masterful use of television and all the teacherly arts. The few can now create, rapidly, new Opinion so that we can make a proper marriage with the planet instead of an incontent rape, in the name of dominion."

—Gore Vidal, from *The United States*

Okay, so you seem to know it all. What books do you go to for guidance?

When it comes to clothes info, I'm a big fan of Alan Flusser, a style maven and clothing designer who's the author of three books, *Making the Man, Clothes and the Man*, and *Style and the Man*. Flusser has his own department at Saks Fifth Avenue, and he's a great adviser on tailoring and great places to shop. And if you need to know how to tie a tie, his books will help you. I'm not going to. As a closet anal-retentive homemaker, my bible and joke book is *How to Do Almost Everything* by Bert Bacharach (Simon and Schuster, 1970). Just try to find that one. This Bert is the father of the famous Burt, the composer. It's a hoot, and where else are you going to learn that the best way to clean your chopping block is with white vinegar? When it comes to cooking there's *Essentials of Classic Italian Cooking* by Marcella Hazan (Knopf, 1992) and *The Rogers and Gray Italian Country Cookbook* by Rose Gray and Ruth Rogers (Random House, 1996).

For other kinds of guidance I go to Wyndham Lewis, Jack Kerouac, William Burroughs, Brion Gysin, Donald Barthelme, Robert

Benchley, Ishmael Reed, William Blake, Oscar Wilde, William Shake-speare, Herodotus, Ovid, Gore Vidal, Ezra Pound, James Purdy, Arthur Rimbaud, and Nathaniel Hawthorne, not to mention Zippy the Pinhead.

For other kinds of guidance I go to Duke Ellington, Miles Davis, Charlie Parker, John Coltrane, Bill Evans, Thelonious Monk, Charles Mingus, Bud Powell, Gil Evans, Charlie Christian, Lee Konitz, Lennie Tristano, Rahsaan Roland Kirk, Bob Dylan, Bob Marley, and Leonard Cohen, not to mention Tom Waits and Lord Buckley.

Why do people consult you for information when all you give is commonsense answers and answers that any ten-year-old can give? Why you?

Aside from the wit and wisdom? Maybe common sense isn't that common. Have you tried Dear Abby or the Playboy Advisor?

Are questions to Style Guy anonymous automatically, or should we state that we want to remain anonymous in our letter?

As you can see, Kyle, readers' letters are always printed anonymously.

Bibliography

Boyer, G. Bruce. *Elegance: A Guide to Quality in Menswear.* New York: Norton, 1985.

Bruce, Lenny. *How to Talk Dirty and Influence People: An Autobiography.* Chicago: Playboy Press, 1965.

Calasibetta, Charlotte Mankey, Ph.D. *Fairchild's Dictionary of Fashion.* 2nd ed. New York: Fairchild Publications, 1988.

Flusser, Alan. *Clothes and the Man: The Principles of Fine Men's Dress.* New York: Villard Books, 1985.

————. *Style and the Man: How and Where to Buy Fine Men's Clothes.* New York: HarperStyle, 1996.

Post, Emily. *Etiquette.* New and rev. ed. New York and London: Funk & Wagnalls, 1927.

Sherwood, Mrs. John. *Manners and Social Usages.* New and rev. ed. New York: Harper & Brothers Publishers, 1897.

Warhol, Andy. *The Philosophy of Andy Warhol: From A to B and Back Again.* New York: Harcourt Brace Jovanovich, 1975.

About the Author

GLENN O'BRIEN writes monthly columns for *Paper* magazine and *GQ*. He was an editor at *Interview*, *Rolling Stone*, and *Spin*. He also wrote the *Interview* column "Glenn O'Brien's Beat" for many years, as well as a column in *Art Forum* and *Details* magazines. He lives in New York City and Bridgehampton, New York.